Desirable Locations

LEICESTER'S MIDDLE CLASS SUBURBS 1880 - 1920

BY
HELEN BOYNTON AND GRANT PITCHES

Cover photograph: The Hermitage, Oadby c. 1920
(Jim Browett)

Published by Leicester City Council
Living History Unit

ISBN 1 901156 00 1

CONTENTS

ACKNOWLEDGEMENTS

One of the pleasures of compiling a book of this nature is renewing and establishing contacts with a wide range of people: property owners, architects, builders, academics and authors. We wish to thank the following, without whom this publication would not have been possible:

Dr Jean Alexander, British Geological Society; John Aston; Roger Barrett; B. H. Bedingfield; Elwyn Bowles; J. N. Brankin-Frisby; Simon Brett; Jim and Margaret Browett; Jenny Burt; Joan Burton; Sid Cadle; Mariolina Clarke and the late John Clarke; Dr Robert Colls; Nicholas Corah; Graham Cousins; John Dixey; Professor Ansel Dunham; George Duxbury; John Eaton; the late Bernard Elliott; Dr Glyn Evans; Neil and Joan Fairley; Jean Farquhar; W. J. M.Fergusson; Harry Gee; Richard Gill; Anthony and Annette Goddard; Herald and Joan Goddard; Michael and Suzy Goddard; Michael Goodhart of Pick Everard Architects; Dr Gornall, Curator Leicester University Botanic Garden; Elizabeth Halford; Ron Hardy; Basil Harrison; Jean Leslie Herbert, Swithland; Audrey Hewitt; Dr and Mrs Hubner; R. P. Boyd James; Gwyn Jones; Jeremy Josephs; Roger Keene; Sylvia Keene; Anthony Kellett; Margaret and Mick King; Dr Pat Kirkham; Cecily Lankester; Eberhard Luithlen; Dr Lutz and Jennifer Luithlen; Dr Alan McWhirr; Lady Martin; Nancy Maxwell; Ben Moffatt; Martin Mortimer; George Newton; John Nisbet, Senior Partner, Pick Everard; Leslie Orton; Pauline Osband, Kirby Muxloe Women's Institute; Sue Parkes and Moira Smith, De Montfort University; Mary Pearce; Barry Pierce-Brown; Professor and Mrs J. C. Pooley; Ray Rayner; Dr John Rice; Dr Judith Roberts; Paul Roberts; Dr Richard Rodger; Paul Rogatzki; George Roper; Arthur Sadler; Jack Sawday and Christopher Sawday; Shirley Scott; Derek Seaton; Len Lloyd Smith; Michael Smith, Birstall; Dr Susan Stevens, Director of Estates and Buildings, De Montfort University; Dr Aubrey Stewart; Ken Stimpson; Dr A. J. Strachan; Dr S. W. J. Theophilus; Christopher Thistlewaite and family; Philip Thornton; Keith and Margaret Torrance; Peter Upton; Wendy Warren; F. B. Wheatcroft; Keith Wheeler; Veronica Orson Wright; Ray Young. Thanks are also due to Cynthia Brown of the Living History Unit, and Kim Pereira, Creativity Works, both of Leicester City Council, for editing the text and preparing it for publication.

PREFACE

Leicester is a very pleasant city. For the most part, its centre has not been disfigured by too many crass developments in the 1950s and 60s, even though there are a few horrors on its edge that are best avoided. But it is the character of many of its suburbs that helps give Leicester a special quality. The middle-classes who created them made sure they were attractive places in which to live. They wanted well-designed houses in spacious, leafy settings which were convenient for work and leisure. Until the motor car made country living feasible for the better off, Leicester's middle-classes lived within the town (or, at least, no further than Oadby or Wigston). Hence, we meet in these pages members of the town's professional and commercial elite who commissioned some of its most impressive houses in some of its most imposing suburbs. Their names may not be generally familiar but in some cases their companies and products are (or were) household names - Goddard's Plate Powder, Dryad, Chilprufe or Stead & Simpson.

Leicester was well-served by local architects who responded to the demands for new houses at the turn of the century, following national trends with flair and imagination. This book takes a close look at these clients, architects and builders, and also explores other aspects like the all important building materials, and the settings of the houses and their gardens. Times change, and social and economic influences have meant profound changes for the suburbs studied here. The movement out of the town, already apparent among the more wealthy in the early part of this century, has escalated; and in any case, modern families no longer have armies of domestic servants to look after them and their houses. Consequently many houses have been turned into flats and student hostels. Listing and the establishment of conservation areas have helped preserve the best of Leicester's middle class suburbs but, as this book concludes, there is more to be done if this fine heritage is to be passed down for future enjoyment.

Geoff Brandwood
May 1996

Grant Pitches 96
'KNIGHTON SPINNEYS'

INTRODUCTION

STATUS, SPACE AND SECURITY

"Architecture is the most pervasive form of History"[1]

The late Victorian suburban villa, in its green setting, embodied some fascinating aspects of the social history as well as the architecture of the period. Built for the rising middle classes from the profits of industry, commerce and the professions, its very variety of form and detail symbolised the values of status, space and security.

Status can be seen as a measure of the "social honour" accorded to an individual, an affirmation of his or her place in the hierarchy of society, expressed in the scale and design of the family home. Space, both inside the house and in its external setting, was testimony not only to personal success, but to the distance which the middle classes strove to put between themselves and the lower orders of society - in terms of lifestyles as well as their physical retreat from the "contagion of the masses", represented by the death, disease and overcrowding of the Victorian city.

Security relates to one of the Victorians' prime social elements: the family, and its key role in society. The family home was a sanctum, embracing a feeling of security and protection from the outside world, but the villa also testified to the new bourgeois roles of the family, especially women, children and domestic servants. In the view of some historians, the middle class can be defined essentially as the "servant-keeping class", and the house was planned to reflect this hierarchy, with designated areas for the family, and the "domestic offices" often located in a separate wing of the house.

Servants had an invisible role, carrying out their duties before the family's breakfast time, and preparing food during the family's leisure time. They were isolated from them by "back stairs", with bedrooms on the top floor, or even in the roof space. In our survey of the selected suburbs, we visited a wide spectrum of houses, from "miniature estates", through large detached houses and terraced villas, to relatively small semi-detached ones. Virtually all incorporated accommodation for servants at this time.

The suburbs of Leicester are particularly rich in this English style of late Victorian and Edwardian dwelling, and their key values can be clearly identified in the physical manifestations of the suburban villa and its setting. Frequently, a focused display of these values was incorporated into the entrance to the main house: a celebration of entrance. Two such entrances, chosen from the Stoneygate East and Oadby suburbs in Leicester and illustrated here, epitomise this approach.

In the Stoneygate example (1879), status is defined by the extravagant use of many materials - the deep banded stone string courses, and tile-hanging, for example. Space is clearly not at a premium in the over-generous porch, and security is implied by the use of heavy-section timber, and double entrance doors.

In the Oadby example, status is defined by the use of a classical pediment and pilasters which frame the entrance, and stained glass windows which are an expensive detail demonstrating the wealth of the owners. The scale of the double height hall beyond is indicated

PORCH DETAIL ARCHITECT J. GODDARD
LONDON ROAD, STONEY GATE

G.K. PITCHES '96

by the stained glass windows. The extravagant use of space beyond the strictly functional need emphasises this value, while the sense of security and enclosure is clearly demonstrated by the double, multi-panelled mahogany doors, made of expensive wood, richly moulded, and heavy in character. Entry beyond this threshold is by invitation only.

The setting of the house was a further dimension of social success: "The status of the area was confirmed to visitors by the space, designed to secure privacy from onlookers".[2] The classic examples of houses in a large-scale setting are in Oadby at Stoughton Drive South, where a series of "miniature estates" was designed by Stockdale Harrison (1846-1914). "Middlemeade" (1904) - now "Beaumont Hall" - is the supreme example of a luxurious Edwardian house in a large well-screened garden.

Security was achieved by the entrance lodge, a prerequisite for large scale houses, together with carefully planned screen planting to the perimeter of the site. The architectural style of these lodges usually matched the "protected" houses, with detailing and ornament of equal quality. Many were essentially functional in purpose, providing accommodation for the head gardener/chauffeur, but they also formed a psychological barrier to the uninvited visitor.

However, the values expressed through architectural style and detail were essentially the outward symbols of a powerful underlying change of culture, which was clearly evident in literature and music as well as architecture during this period. This cultural sea change focused on the notion of "Englishness", in which life in

ENTRANCE DETAIL (1904)
KNIGHTON RISE OADBY
GK PITCHES '90

the country house was symbolic of the ideal values of "English" culture. Two examples of this are John Galsworthy's "The Country House" (1907), which reinforces the mystical values of Old England; and E. M. Forster's "Howard's End" (1910), which has been described as "the symbolic representation of civilised England".[3]

In exploring the middle class suburbs of Leicester, we asked three general questions. Firstly, how did the

Rolls Royce in the drive of
The Hermitage, Oadby
(Helen Boynton)

geology and topography of the region moderate the patterns of settlement? Secondly, which historical factors were important in determining the evolution of the suburbs; and finally, which were the significant architectural practices, and the builders, who were responsible for the superb range of domestic architecture of this period?

The factors involved in suburban development are complex, but three aspects were of particular significance in Leicester: transport systems, land ownership and geographical location. One facet of the expanding rail network in the later 19th century was the opportunity to develop low density housing for businessmen in the suburbs, although it is interesting that Oadby, where there was a concentration of this group, did not have a railway station. The main London to Leicester line by-passed it to the west, but this proved no great obstacle. Its wealthy inhabitants owned horse-drawn carriages and were independent travellers.

In the outer areas of Leicester, stations were opened at South Wigston (1840), Wigston Magna (1854), Kirby Muxloe (1859), Thurnby (1883), and Belgrave, Birstall and Rothley (1899). Horse-drawn trams, introduced in Leicester in 1874, and the electric trams which replaced them 30 years later, also contributed to the development of the urban fringes. However, the role of transport in the evolution of the suburbs is not clear cut. As one historian has suggested, "passenger networks required passengers to generate adequate revenue to operate. Consequently they followed rather than preceded residential development".[4]

Land ownership is one of the most important factors in the development of the suburbs, and the two systems of land tenure - leasehold and freehold - had a crucial impact on the creation of hierarchies of housing. In the case of leasehold land, the landowner could impose restrictions relating to the pattern and layout of the streets, and the uses to which buildings could be put. He or she often commissioned architects who would determine the design policy. Freehold land offered a greater degree of freedom in planning and design, but here too there might be constraints, such as restricted covenants imposed as a condition of sale.

There were major regional differences in terms of land tenure. Birmingham, for instance, was predominantly leasehold, but Leicester's pattern of land ownership was more complex. The south east areas which feature prominently in this book were largely freehold, and they generally offer a great variety of housing styles within each suburb. Additionally they demonstrate variations of wealth and status within the middle class itself, reflected not only in the scale and quality of individual houses and villas, but by the structure and character of their gardens and small estates. Along with the private archives of the Goddard family of architects, sale catalogues produced in the 1920s and 1930s by the former estate agents, Warner, Sheppard and Wade have been particularly valuable sources, providing a fascinating insight into the social priorities of prospective middle class property owners.

The core of this book is an illustrated appraisal of the significant domestic architecture of selected suburbs between about 1880 and 1920. Our selection includes a number of outstanding houses built for prominent Leicester businessmen in outer areas such as Great Glen, Kirby Fields, Woodhouse Eaves and Rothley, but in general we have not covered the inner more familiar areas of the city which have been fully described by a number of other authors. To place the buildings in their proper context, we have included sections on the significance of local topography and geology in the pattern and style of suburban growth, and profiles of some of Leicester's leading architectural practices and builders.

Finally, who were the middle class businessmen whose desire for status, space and security shaped Leicester's suburban development in the later 19th and earlier 20th centuries? There are too many to mention individually here, but we can identify some of their common characteristics.

Apart from iron-founding, hosiery was the only industry of any substance in Leicester until the mid 19th century. From the 1850s, however, footwear manufacture became established in the town, giving a boost in turn to the hosiery by stimulating demand for elastic webbing. In the second half of the century the engineering industry also expanded, initially supplying hosiery and footwear machinery, but later producing such goods as clocks, lifts and optical instruments.

Food and drink, printing, silver polish manufacture, and cigar- and umbrella-making were among a host of smaller industries which were well established by the end of the 19th century. This was one of the most prosperous periods in Leicester's history; and as industrial expansion continued and the economy became more complex, there was a parallel expansion in the service sector, notably in professional occupations. The ranks of the middle classes also embraced solicitors, architects, doctors and others beside, and while they might not accumulate wealth on the scale of the large industrialists, many enjoyed a very comfortable lifestyle.

Most 19th century businesses in Leicester were family firms built up from modest beginnings over two or three generations. Though their founders liked to describe themselves as "self-made" men, most had some previous business experience, and many came from families already engaged in commerce or industry. Harry Peach (1874-1936) was a bookseller in Belvoir Street before founding the Dryad Company in 1907 to produce cane furniture. His friend and mentor Benjamin J. Fletcher, head of the Leicester School of Art, designed the early products while Peach provided the finance. Five years later Peach moved into the field of metalwork, and went into partnership with William Pick of Collins and Co.. Dryad Metal Works produced a wide range of metals goods, from copper water jugs to door furniture.

Samuel Bailey Goodwin and William Barsby, founders of the engineering firm of Goodwin Barsby, were previously foremen at local ironmongery firms, while Nathaniel Corah, who founded the Corah hosiery company in 1815 from a small house in St. Nicholas Street, was the son of a Leicestershire farmer and hosier. After Nathaniel's death, the business was continued by his three sons, John, William and Thomas, whom he had taken into partnership in 1830. They were followed in turn by Thomas's elder son Edwin, and John Harris Cooper, one of Thomas Corah's former apprentices.

The company was one of the earliest in Leicester to apply steam power to the manufacture of hosiery, and hence to shift production from homes and small workshops into the factory. Its purpose built St. Margaret's works, close to the church of the same name, were opened in 1866. In 1883, the "Leicester Post" commended the company's "conspicuous energy" and enterprise in installing electric lighting in its factory, the first in Leicester to be illuminated in this way. Like many other local employers, Corah prided itself on its paternalistic care for its workforce, and its generosity to the wider community - and this particular occasion was celebrated with two parties: one for 1100 guests, employees and their spouses, and the second for over 1000 of the town's "Aged Poor".

The ability to spot a potential market, coupled with enterprise and a willingness to take risks, were characteristic of those businessmen who did prosper. The local footwear retailer Joseph Frisby began his own career selling shoes from a market stall in Chesterfield.

'MIDDLEMEADE' (1904) OADBY
ARCHITECT: STOCKDALE HARRISON

GRANT PITCHER 96

With the help of his two brothers, other stalls were opened and eventually replaced by shops - over 100 branches within 30 years. In due course, Joseph Brankin-Frisby, Joseph's son, married Peggy North, daughter of W. A. North, Chairman of Freeman Hardy and Willis, demonstrating another common characteristic of the Leicester business community - the formation of dynastic families by intermarriage within the same industry, or at least the same social "mileau."

J. Wallis Goddard (1851-1927) was among those businessmen who inherited wealth from earlier generations of the family. His grandfather was a banker, and his father Joseph a chemist who founded an international business on the manufacture of non-mercurial silver plate powder. Wallis Goddard was articled to the eminent architect George Gilbert Scott, but gave up architecture to join his father's rapidly expanding business. Like many local businessmen, he was something of a benefactor, and sold a large site near Avenue Road for a nominal sum to the Leicestershire Lawn Tennis Club - on condition that no alcohol was consumed on the premises, and no tennis was played on Sundays.

J. Wallis Goddard c.1925, and sale brochure (Herald Goddard)

Goddard's Plate Powder
Sold in Boxes - 1/-, 2/6 & 7/6

Less typically, he also supported a number of young businessmen in various enterprises, some of which grew into international companies. They included the Imperial Typewriter Co., Wadkin Ltd., manufacturers of wood-working machinery, and the Bentley Engineering Co..

Another factor J. Wallis Goddard had in common with many of his middle class contemporaries in Leicester was religious nonconformity, which was often allied politically to the Liberal cause. Goddard contributed to the building of Stoneygate Baptist Church on London Road, while John Adams Bolton (1868-1945), founder of the clothing firm Chilprufe and the son of a doctor, is an interesting example of a man whose relations with his employees were informed by his own religious beliefs. He was once employed in the finishing department of Ernest Walker, hosiery manufacturer, where he developed a particular interest in the chemistry of fibres. Though he had no formal scientific education, he invented a new washing process for woollen garments, from which the "Chilprufe" company derived its name.

A staunch Methodist, John Bolton worshipped at Melbourne Hall, which for many years

operated a prison-gate mission to discharged prisoners - several of whom were employed by Chilprufe. In summer, recalled his former chauffeur Ernest Bull, he invited his workers and their families to swim in the lake at his home, "Tetuan" in Manor Road, Oadby, where paddle boats were provided. Unusually, he also introduced a profit-sharing scheme for employees (they also shared the losses in times of poor trade, on one occasion by accepting a 10% reduction in wages), and encouraged them to offer suggestions for improving efficiency.

By the earlier 20th century, most companies of any size in Leicester were providing their workers with recreational and sporting facilities, annual outings and other benefits "in kind". These were designed to promote a healthier and thus more efficient workforce, as well as a sense of loyalty to the employer - which might be seen as a form of insurance against working class discontent. However, whatever the denomination, religious conviction also encouraged a strong commitment to public service among local businessmen and their families, whether through membership of various local government bodies or patronage of charities. Wives and daughters were particularly active in such suitably "feminine" areas as infant and maternal welfare, education and poor relief.

Among the most notable individual acts of philanthropy during this period was Thomas Fielding Johnson's gift of six acres of land and the former County Lunatic Asylum building for use as a University College

after the First World War. A further £100,000 was given to support the venture within the space of 18 months. Johnson had taken over the flourishing business of his uncle Joseph on the death of the latter in the 1850s, and was succeeded in turn by his own son Thomas Junior (1856 - 1931).

The social and philanthropic activities of Leicester's middle classes were not of course entirely disinterested. As employers, as Justices of the Peace, members of the Poor Law Board, the Leicester School Board and the Borough Council, and as patrons of a host of local charities and cultural organisations, they were able to wield a formidable amount of power and influence over the lives of its citizens. Though they had migrated to the suburbs, they remained as visible and as involved as ever in the life of the town; but the fine houses they occupied were the outward manifestation of their status and success, paid for and if need by justified by hard work, the risks involved in making money, and a "giving back" through public service to the community in which they had prospered.

References

1. Caption from R.I.B.A. exhibition "Strangely Familiar", March 1996
2. Long H., The Edwardian House (1993)
3. Border P. & .Widdowson P., "A Literature of England" in Colls R. & Dodd P., ed. Englishness: Politics and Culture 1880-1920 (1986)
4. Rodger R., Housing in Britain 1780-1914 (1989), p. 39

'SUMMER HILL'
LETCHWORTH ROAD LEICESTER
ARCHITECT : R.W. BEDINGFIELD (1872 - 1940)

GRANT PILCHES '96

THE TOPOGRAPHY AND GEOLOGY OF LEICESTER AND LEICESTERSHIRE

"The subject of Material is clearly the foundation of architecture"[1]

Leicester occupies a central position in the county, with a network of roads and railways radiating from it. There was a Celtic settlement here before the Roman town of Ratae Corieltauvorum was established, where the river was bridged, and the town subsequently developed outwards away from the flood plain of the Soar to the higher surrounding land.

The suburbs described in this book have grown up on good well-drained soils, firstly of the river terraces with their spring-lines, and then on the higher sunnier and drier areas, away from the river valley which was liable to flooding, and to damp polluted fogs and mists in winter. The highest point in the city (102 metres) is on its eastern side, near Spencefield Lane, Evington.

Domestic buildings in Leicester and its suburbs greatly reflect the local building materials taken from quarries or pits in the city and county. The oldest rocks in Leicestershire outcrop in Charnwood Forest to the north west and belong to the Precambrian system. They consist of slates and igneous rocks, such as the pinkish-green diorites of Markfield, all of which were used during the late Victorian and Edwardian period in Leicester's houses.

The Swithland slates in particular, quarried from Swithland Woods, The Brand and Groby, were excellent for roofs and hung tiles. The nature of the natural cleavage, which allowed splitting in a vertical plane, ensured that blocks could be cut easily into tiles. The roofing slates are highly prized today, but are expensive to replace. The close texture, lack of porosity, and thus the waterproof nature and resistance to frost meant they have been capable of withstanding weathering.

Swithland slates have a greenish tinge, due to the mineral chlorite. This makes them particularly attractive compared with the purplish-grey of the machine-cut slates from North Wales, which were used extensively in Leicester in the later 19th century.

Moving up the geological column, Carboniferous Limestone outcrops as fairly small exposures in north west Leicestershire, particularly at Breedon Cloud and Breedon Hill quarries. Very few buildings in Leicester show this grey-white, attractive and relatively hard-wearing stone, although it was used for rockery gardens in some of the largest suburban houses. Above the Carboniferous Limestone is the Millstone Grit, which consists of variably coloured quartz-rich sandstones of yellowish, brownish and pinkish hues, which are used as quoins, mullions and transoms in some houses.

This formation outcrops locally only in north west Leicestershire, adjacent to the county boundary near Melbourne. These sandstones were more extensively quarried from Derbyshire and Yorkshire. The latter produced the well-known York flags, which are fine-grained and split relatively easily along the bedding planes to produce "flagstones", used for patios in some of the larger gardens - that of "Middlemeade", for instance, in Stoughton Drive South.

The Coal Measures which follow upwards are exposed in the Leicestershire coalfield around Coalville, Ibstock and Ashby, and have yielded fire clays and clays which have been used for brick making. Ibstock brick is a beige-biscuit coloured brick which can be seen in a number of Leicester houses, including "Thornleigh" (1871) on London Road. Bricks made at a number of brickyards in this part of the county were used in Leicester's Victorian and Edwardian suburbs.

Above the Coal Measures comes the Trias system. This is extensively exposed in Leicestershire from its western boundary to a line which runs through Victoria Park and across London Road, just east of the River Soar. The Daneshill sandstones of Triassic age are pinkish-buff in colour and came from small quarries in the Dane Hills area of West Leicester. They can still be seen outcropping in Western Park, and in the railway cutting of the Shoulder of Mutton Hill on Hinckley Road. They are very attractively used as lintels, mullions, quoins and transoms in some of the larger houses.

Letchworth Road was developed on a ridge of the sandstone overlooking Western Park, while Ashleigh Road and Westcotes Drive were developed on a similar smaller ridge in the Westcotes area. These sandstone ridges, albeit quite local, have provided well-drained sunny sites for building. The individual small quartz grains can often be picked out, and building stones may show curved current bedding, indicating that the sands were laid down by current action in shallow seas which covered much of the area in the Triassic period.

The red Mercia Mudstones (Keuper Marls) of the Trias system played a very important part in giving Leicester its distinctive appearance as a red brick city. Reddish brown bricks have been made throughout Leicestershire from these marls (limy clays), and small brick pits were first opened in the Highfields/Regent Road/Knighton railway junction areas during the Victorian period. These pits gradually closed down as the marl became exhausted and new brick pits opened

further out, in Gipsy Lane, Humberstone (New Star Brick Pit) and Sileby, for instance. However, these too have now closed down.

Bricks fired from the Keuper Marl have weathered over the decades to a warm orange-red hue, as iron is oxidised on exposure, but the facing bricks of many houses built near the turn of the century show very little actual weathering and are almost as good as they were 100 years ago. Bricks made at this time were slightly larger than those of today, and many came from the brickyards at Woodville, near Ashby, and Ellistown, near Coalville. These bricks can be identified by the name of the brickyard, and in the case of the latter, by the Ellistown bell in the indentations on the surface, known as "frogs". They were used in the building of many of the large houses – "Nether Close", Oadby for example – and their garden walls. White gypsum from the Keuper Marl of the Gipsy Lane brickworks can also be found in many old rockeries in the gardens of smaller houses.

The Trias is followed upwards by the Jurassic system, and the boundary between the two actually forms the hill up London Road to Victoria Park. In Leicester itself, the lowest Jurassic rocks to be exposed are the Lower Lias clays which can often be seen in building excavations, particularly around the Gartree Road/Evington Brook areas, where dark grey blue clays containing fossil oysters and brachiopod shells have been found. Above the Lower Lias clays is a succession of ironstones, limestones and clays which cover most of eastern Leicestershire. The limestones have been particularly important as building stones in Leicester as quoins, mullions, transoms, string courses and lintels.

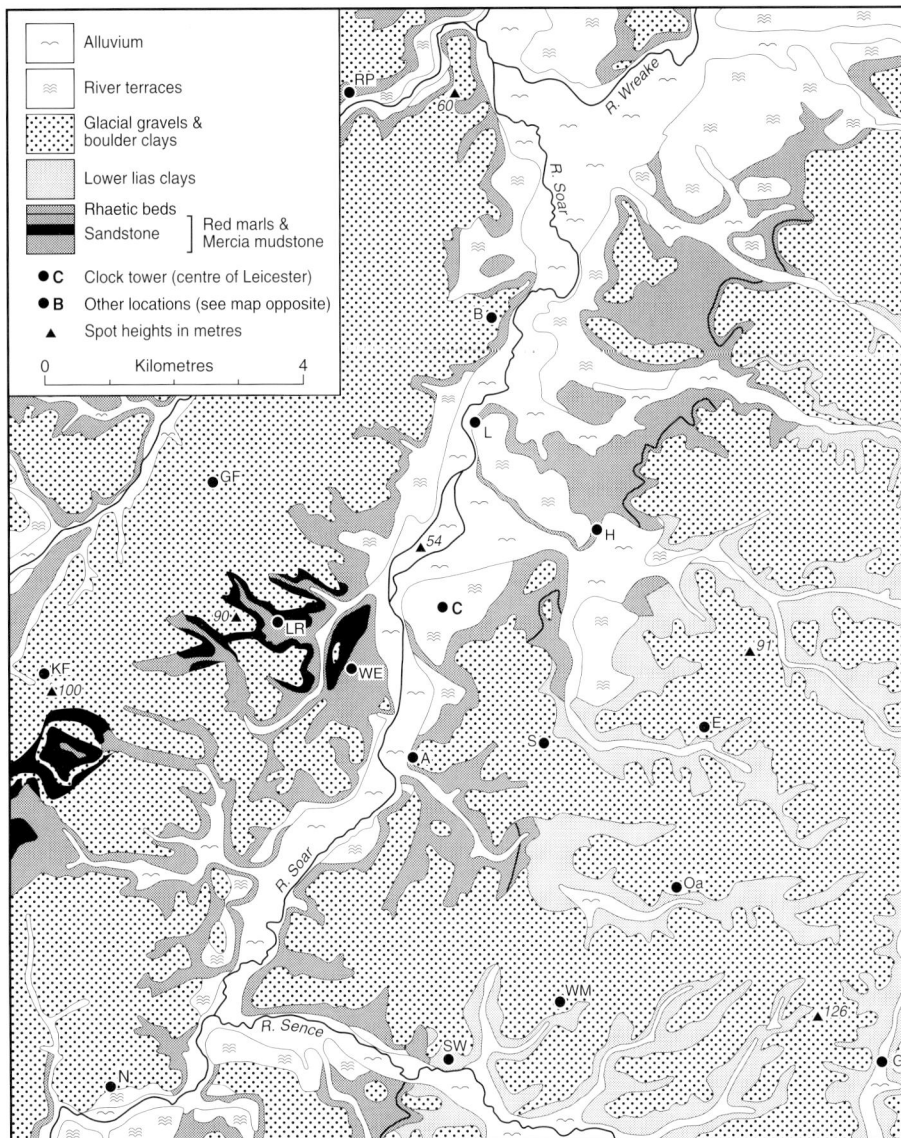

Legend:

- ～ Alluvium
- ≋ River terraces
- Glacial gravels & boulder clays
- Lower lias clays
- Rhaetic beds ⎤ Red marls &
- Sandstone ⎦ Mercia mudstone
- ● C Clock tower (centre of Leicester)
- ● B Other locations (see map opposite)
- ▲ Spot heights in metres

0   Kilometres   4

**Geological map of Leicester and its environs
(Reproduced by permission of British Geological Society)**

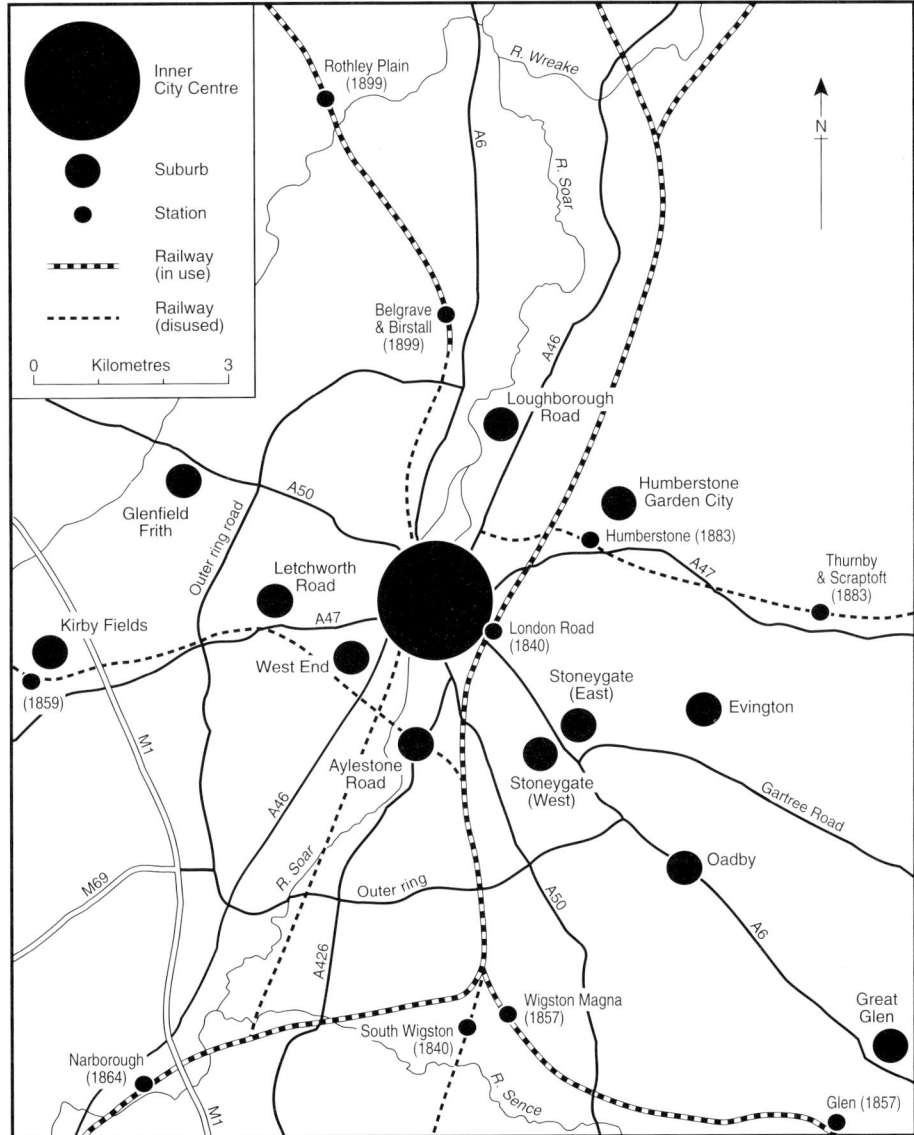

Inner City Centre

Suburb

Station

Railway (in use)

Railway (disused)

0   Kilometres   3

Rothley Plain (1899)

R. Wreake

A6

R. Soar

A46

Belgrave & Birstall (1899)

Loughborough Road

Humberstone Garden City

Humberstone (1883)

A47

Thurnby & Scraptoft (1883)

Glenfield Frith

A50

Outer ring road

Letchworth Road

A47

West End

London Road (1840)

Kirby Fields

(1859)

M1

A46

Stoneygate (East)

Evington

Aylestone Road

Stoneygate (West)

Gartree Road

R. Soar

Outer ring

A50

Oadby

A6

M69

A426

Wigston Magna (1857)

Great Glen

South Wigston (1840)

R. Sence

Narborough (1864)

M1

Glen (1857)

Location of suburbs
(Reproduced by permission of British Geological Society)

Four varieties of limestone were used: oolitic, which contains small spherical ooliths of calcium carbonate; iron stained limestone with the mineral limonite, which gives the rock a golden brown tint; shelly limestone with fossil fragments; and pure cream coloured fine-grained even-textured limestones. These various limestones came mostly from quarries on the Leicestershire border, including Clipsham and Ketton. They have weathered fairly well over the decades, except where the grain size is large and the shelly fragments numerous, or if the blocks were positioned in a direction which was not in line with the natural bedding plane direction. The closer the grain and the more "correct" the alignment of the blocks, the better the preservation of the structure of the houses.

Finally, the Pleistocene period at the top of the geological column is represented by sands, clays and boulder clays, laid down by the ice sheets which advanced down from the north in four successive stages over Great Britain to a southerly position approximately on the line of the River Thames. Leicestershire is covered by a discontinuous outcrop of these beds, which give rise to generally well drained soils. Boulder clay is greyish blue when unweathered but becomes browner on exposure to the air. It gives a firm foundation for building, and when weathered, a fertile if somewhat heavy, loamy soil. Stoneygate has grown up on such a ridge of glacial clays and stony soils, and London Road follows this ridge south east into the county.[2]

References
1. William Morris address to the Arts Workers' Guild, January 1882.
2. For further information on the geology of Leicestershire, see Pye N. ed., Leicester and its Region (1972).

LATE-VICTORIAN VILLAS
EAST STONEYGATE LEICESTER

GRANT PITCHES '94

ARCHITECTURAL PRACTICES AND BUILDING FIRMS

"The growth of the professions... brought with it more expert – and specialised – knowledge..."[1]

At the beginning of the 19th century, architects were perceived as a low income group, often tainted by corruption. Their status changed over the course of the century, and by the late Victorian period architecture had become an established and respectable profession. One reason for its earlier bad image was the close association of architects with the building trade, and their consequent lack of independent judgement -

although there were many who operated with integrity within the embryonic profession.

The Institute of Architects was founded in 1834, and awarded a Royal Charter three years later. At that time the fundamental purposes of R.I.B.A. were "to promote the domestic convenience of citizens, and the public improvement and embellishment of towns and cities". The professionalisation of architects, following the formulation of a training policy and legal recognition of their status, helped to change their image, accountability and income. Local architects were influenced to varying degrees by the work of significant national practitioners. Among the most potent means of influencing ideas and disseminating information were the art magazines and professional journals of the mid and late Victorian periods, which provided a full spectrum of comment on architecture of the day, and at the same time profiled its leading exponents. Chronologically they included The Builder (founded in 1842), The Studio (1893), Country Life (1897), and the Architectural Review.

Under the editorship of George Godwin, The Builder provided not only design and technical information, but alerted its readers to social issues such as slum overcrowding. The Studio, which was also circulated in Europe, was instrumental in popularising the work of the Arts and Crafts movement, and that of C. F. A. Voysey, one of the leading architects of the day. Country Life, founded by Edward Hudson, did much to promote the work of the architect Edwin Lutyens, but was unique in that it catered for a wealthy and middle class readership.

Where they are discernible, we trace the influence of national architects on the style, form and detail of the suburban houses that we analyse in this book. At this point it will be useful to identify salient design characteristics of the three most influential national practitioners during this period: Norman Shaw, C. F. A. Voysey, and Baillie Scott.

Norman Shaw (1831-1912) is perceived by many architectural historians as the most influential of the Arts and Crafts architects. Shaw's work is characterised by his "Old English" style which he developed from his study of English vernacular buildings, and subsequently a style based on the architecture of 17th and 18th century England – the so called "Queen Anne Style". His eclectic architecture, combining tile-hanging, or half-timbering on the first floor with brick or stonework on the ground floor, was highly influential on architects. Leicester practitioners who developed and modified this style included Stockdale Harrison, whose spectacular houses on Oadby and Stoneygate will be examined later.

By contrast, "Horizontalism" was the pervading aspect of the work of C. F. A. Voysey (1857-1941): a combination of economy, horizontal space (low ceilings) and beautifully detailed materials. Voysey's white rough-cast walls and slate roofs, a potent contrast of materials, were adopted as a theme by many architects and speculative builders in Britain and Europe. M. H. Baillie Scott (1865-1945) had a significant influence on the design of the small detached house. His contribution was the development of the "integrated interior". In planning terms, he opened up the hall from a single cell into a space from which other rooms, dining and sitting, were linked. He was an exponent of "Free Design" in which experiments in the use of materials were pursued. The overriding aim of his design approach was to create a feeling of repose, and a "homogeneous atmosphere". He also designed the furniture for a large number of his buildings.

These great national architects provided an influential range of design precedents for provincial architects. Their buildings, which were widely published in the professional journals, were analysed by architects in stylistic and detail terms. These can be seen to have influenced the nature of architecture developed by Leicester's leading practices over this period. The following are profiles of some of the practices most closely involved in the development of Leicester's middle class suburbs.

Architectural practices

Isaac Barradale

Isaac Barradale (1845-1892) is known in particular for his pioneering use of the English Revival style, and his work features strongly in any survey of 19th and early 20th century buildings in Leicester. Barradale was articled to the local architect William Flint (1801-1862) and set up his practice in Leicester in 1870. Barradales's most famous building is probably Fenwick's department store, formerly Joseph Johnson's, at the corner of Belvoir Street and Market Street, but he was also responsible for a number of superb terraced villas in Stoneygate.

Ralph Waldo Bedingfield

Ralph Waldo Bedingfield A.R.I.B.A. (1872-1940), was born in Bristol on 30 July 1872, and served his articles with Goddard, Paget and Goddard of Leicester. A keen gardener and traveller, he specialised in domestic

'HALF BUTTERFLY' HOUSE
MEADOW COURT ROAD OADBY (PLANS DEPOSITED 1913 & 1919)
ARCHITECT A. E AND T SAWDAY

architecture, and also taught at the Leicester School of Architecture for several years. He lived initially in Stoneygate Road, but moved in 1925 to Gullet Lane, Kirby Muxloe, and subsequently to Kirby Fields. His office was at 9 The Crescent, King Street, Leicester.

Bedingfield was clearly influenced by the work of C. F. A. Voysey. The two houses he designed at Kirby Fields in the late twenties, "Ringwood" for himself, and "White Cottage" on the adjacent plot, have hints of

Voisey's white rough-cast walls and heavy roof forms. "Glebe House", Oadby has several features which are clearly reminiscent of Voysey, particularly the beautiful eaves brackets and window details.

Everard Pick

The founder of what was to develop as one of the largest practices in the East Midlands was John Breedon Everard, a civil engineer and architect. Through his personal links with Edward Shipley Ellis, later Chairman of the Midland Railway, he gained an engineering position with the new St. Pancras Station. Everard eventually returned to Leicester, and set up a practice in 1867. At the age of 27 he won a major competition for the new Leicester Cattle Market on Aylestone Road, which effectively launched his firm. He remained a partner until 1911.

The architect partner of the firm, who became the Leicestershire County Architect and Engineer for fifty years, was Samuel Perkins Pick. He joined Everard as an assistant in 1882, and was a partner between 1888-1919. His most famous design is probably Thomas Pares' Bank (1900) in St. Martin's, now the National Westminster. By the turn of the century, Pick had established the firm's links with the County Council (founded in 1889), and the Governors of the Leicester Infirmary, the foundation of a very important group of clients. The partnership of Everard and Pick was later expanded to include Bernard Everard (1905-1923) and William Keay (1911-1952).

The most significant feature of this remarkable firm was that it was multidisciplinary - virtually a pioneering concept for this period. As well as architectural work such as hospitals and the Technical and Art Schools, the practice designed sewage disposal and water works, reservoirs and other public works. This resulted in a wide range of projects, as the role of the public authorities widened. Perkins Pick, in common with many architects of his generation, rejected the Gothic style of the High Victorian period, and adopted a range of styles depending on the building type. His Pares Bank in St. Martins was in the Classical Baroque style, whereas his domestic work reflected the emerging popularity of the "vernacular revival" or "Old English" style brilliantly developed by Norman Shaw. An excellent example of this is "The Coppice" (1910) on the corner of Manor Road and Stoughton Drive South in Oadby. Its double-bay gabled main facade with the black and white half-timbering typifies this style.

Significant Houses refurbished by Everard Pick included "Woodville" (1893) on Knighton Park Road for J.B. Everard; "Buckhurst" (1909) and "The Oaks" (1910) on London Road, both demolished; "The Woodlands" (1910) on Knighton Road (demolished); and "Knighton Lodge" (1923) in Elms Road.

The Goddards

This was one of the most significant practices in Leicester from the early Victorian to the late Edwardian period. Founded by Henry Goddard (1813-1899) in the 1830s, the firm eventually spanned six generations of architects, including Joseph Goddard, designer of Leicester's Clock Tower (1868) and the Leicestershire Bank (now the Midland Bank) in Granby Street (1874). A

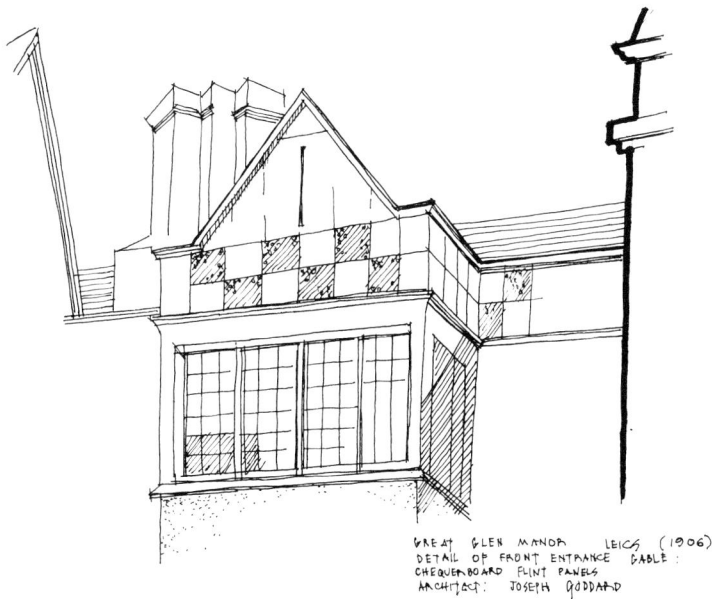

GREAT GLEN MANOR LEICS (1906)
DETAIL OF FRONT ENTRANCE GABLE:
CHEQUERBOARD FLINT PANELS
ARCHITECT: JOSEPH GODDARD

It can be argued that it is this attention to detail of both the building fabric and the interior elements which gives the work of the Goddard practice its special quality.

Lawton Brown and Jones

The founder of the firm was George Lawton Brown (1868-1934) who was born in Leicester, and educated at Tenby. After serving his articles, he started his own practice about 1890. His long association with Percy C. Jones started when the latter was articled to him in 1898, and joined him as a partner to form Lawton Brown and Jones in 1910. The firm was responsible for a wide range of commercial buildings, churches and houses in Leicester, including "The Spinneys" on Manor Road.

In the context of domestic architecture, there is a modest hint of the Queen Anne Revival style in some of the house designs: for example, the Dutch gables featured in a house in Great Glen, Leicestershire, an example of Shaw's influence. Overall, however, the domestic work is not flamboyant. Lawton Brown was said to have "a retiring disposition, and did not take any prominent part in public life, but his work and influence were carried out with quiet efficiency…" (L.R.S.A. obituary 1934).

A.E. and T. Sawday

Compared to the large firm of Everard Pick this was a medium sized practice, but it was a significant one. Albert Edwin Sawday was born in Sidmouth, Devon in 1851. After leaving school, was articled to a London firm of architects, and settled in Leicester around 1872. The

definitive analysis of the Goddards' architectural practice is given in Brandwood and Cherry's book "Men of Property: the Goddards and six generations of architects" (1990). In the context of domestic work in the suburbs, some of the most spectacular examples are to be found in Stoneygate. "Knighton Spinneys" (1885-6) in Ratcliffe Road, designed by Joseph Goddard for his own occupation, is a particularly exuberant example.

Brandwood and Cherry suggest that H.L. Goddard's arrival in the practice as a partner in 1888 was decisive. The sketches he produced on his study trips to Europe concentrated on "decorative details", and an examination of the rich collection of drawings in the Goddard archive reveals an intense involvement with detail. Many of the projects include full-size drawings of such diverse elements as chimney-stack brick-bonding to weather vanes.

practice was founded in 1878 as Redfern and Sawday. Albert Sawday became active in local politics, serving as a Liberal councillor for many years, and as Mayor in 1903.

The firm carried out a number of commercial commissions but its speciality was the small detached house for the middle class client. Meadowcourt Road, Oadby (laid out in 1910) is a good example of a range of houses, well detailed, with varying plan forms including the "half butterfly" - a variation on the "butterfly" plan devised by E.S. Prior (1852-1932) to emphasise a house visually as shelter. The houses are characterised by predominant gables to the road facades, rendered or with vertical tiles, and sensitively detailed features such as entrance doors and surrounds. There are echoes of Voysey in some of the houses with their white rendered walls and tall chimneys.

Stockdale Harrison and Sons

Along with the Goddards, Stockdale Harrison and Sons was one of the two major dynastic architectural firms operating in Leicester during the Victorian and Edwardian periods. Its best known public buildings included the Leicester Working Men's College in Great Central Street, the Vestry Street baths, and De Montfort Hall. However, some of the finest houses built in the Leicester suburbs were designed by Stockdale Harrison and his sons Shirley and James.

Stockdale Harrison F.R.I.B.A. (1846-1914) was born in Leicester, and articled in 1862 to the local architect James Bird. He moved to London six years later, and on his return to Leicester in 1870 started his own practice with his former schoolfriend Isaac Barradale. Stockdale's two sons, Shirley Harrison A.R.I.B.A (1880-1961) and James, joined him around the turn of the century, and had some influence on his design approach. James, however, was very much involved in developing a strong client base, and less concerned with design issues.

Shirley's first house was a low budget commission in 1909 from Mr I. Kirk, manager of the Beaumanor estate, on a site in Woodhouse Eaves. His most famous house is probably "Four Gables" in Elms Road, Leicester which he designed for himself in 1910 in the highly romantic Arts and Crafts style, which undoubtedly influenced the thematic style of the firm. From the turn of the century to the early 1930s, when the Modernist Movement was beginning to gain credence in Britain, the domestic work of Stockdale Harrison and Sons was characterised by an eclectic style based on the sensitive use of traditional technology and materials: brick, tile, half-timbering and tile-hanging.

Stockdale Harrison and Sons have left a rich heritage of very fine houses of the late Victorian and Edwardian period in Oadby and Stoneygate, and some of these are described in a later section. Several have been converted to use as University halls of residence, and are a microcosm of the greatest domestic work of this firm, together with that of the Goddards, and R. W. Bedingfield.

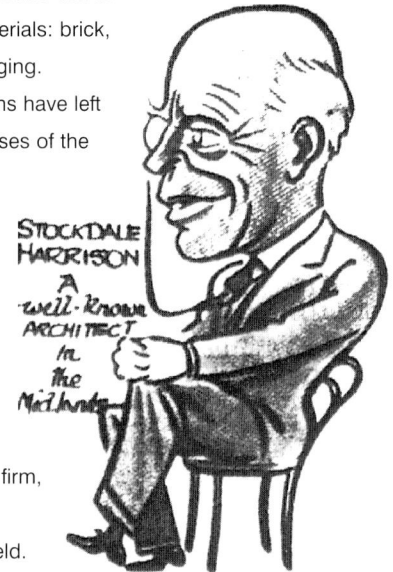

STOCKDALE HARRISON A well-known ARCHITECT in the Midlands

Building firms

The dramatic increase in the population of Leicester from about 122,000 in 1881 to 234,000 in 1921 was reflected in the pattern of building. Churches, banks, hospitals and educational buildings were designed and built by Leicester's leading architects and builders. Over this period there was inevitably a housing boom - the number built virtually doubled from about 25,000 to 43,000, despite the virtual cessation of house building during the First World War.

In the suburbs of Kirby Fields, Oadby, and Stoneygate large detached houses were being built for the rapidly expanding middle class population. However, while the names of the leading architectural practices may be well known, those of the builders themselves are perhaps less familiar. Five building firms were particularly active in a wide range of building types over this period: Henry Herbert and Sons; J C Kellett; Duxbury and Sons; Stimpson and Rolleston; and George Hewitt and Sons. Between them they may have accounted for as much as a third to a half of the building work in the suburbs discussed in this book. Also worth noting is Broadbents Limited, one of the most important builders' merchant at this time, which specialised in roofing.

Broadbents Limited

The business was formed in Horsefair Street, Leicester, in 1840 by Benjamin Broadbent (1813-62) and William Hawley, but the partnership was dissolved about 1856. Broadbent traded initially as a sculptor, mason and architect, and one of his notable early works was the building of Anstey Church. The founder was succeeded by his son Benjamin, who at the age of 21 had become a partner in a timber firm in Erskine Street, with a Mr Robinson and Jacob Staveley, clayware manufacturers at Nuneaton. The three partners continued to develop their interests but diversified into timber and joinery from Scandinavia and Russia.

In the late 19th century a significant part of the firm's business was slate.

SLATING AND TILING.

Prices per square, or lump Sum to Architects' Quantities for work fixed complete in any part of the Country with

SLATES. Dinorwic, Bangor, Carnarvon' Portmadoc, Westmorland-Green, Sedan-Green, Imperial-Green, Grey-Green, Slates, &c.

TILES. Broseley, Staffordshire, Yorkshire, Bridgewater, Asbestos, &c.

SEND PARTICULARS OR QUANTITIES TO

BROADBENT & STEPHENS

LEICESTER also WORTHING and LUTON

Wholesale Slate Merchants.

LARGE STOCKS KEPT OF ALL KINDS AND SIZES OF SLATES.
PROMPT DELIVERY. EXPERIENCED WORKMEN.

Also MANUFACTURERS of

SANITARY PIPES and Connections, Gulleys, Sinks, Chimney Pots, Fire Bricks.

ILLUSTRATED CATALOGUE AND PRICES ON APPLICATION.
Telegrams : "BROADBENT'S, Leicester." ESTABLISHED 1840. Telephone No. 5048

It acted as main agents for Lord Penrhyn Quarry, first as suppliers but later as slating and tiling contractors. This work included some prestigious projects such as St. John's College, Cambridge (1892), the Albermarle Hotel, Piccadilly (1897), and locally, the Pearson and Bennion Factory (1897), later the British United Shoe Machinery Co.. The First World War had a fundamental impact on Broadbents' labour force, as a large number of men joined up, and the company's horses were commandeered by the Army. However, following the death of Stanley Broadbent in 1915, the business was continued by his widow. It later traded as Broadbent and Stephens, with other branches in Worthing and Luton. Today, Broadbents (Leicester) Ltd. is a large scale national business.

G Duxbury & Sons Limited

The firm was founded about 1840 by Thomas Duxbury (1815-87). It was developed by George (1855-1922) and George Thomas Duxbury, and maintained its momentum up to the early 1990s, trading under various Duxbury names. Thomas Duxbury - "T. D." - undertook a range of "quality work" and built a number of sizeable detached houses, an example of which was "The Osiers" on the Soar bridge at Cossington. Around 1900, George Duxbury - "G. D." - moved the works around 1900 from Northampton Street to 73 Churchgate, and

HENRY HERBERT & SONS
ESTABLISHED OVER 100 YEARS.
BUILDERS
33 MILLSTONE LANE, LEICESTER
Telephone : LEICESTER 21734

ALSO ALTERATIONS & REPAIRS IN ALL BRANCHES OF THE TRADE. CITY & COUNTY

Advertisements (above and preceding page) from Kelly's "Directory of Leicestershire and Rutland" (1932)

built the adjacent "Hasledene". He was primarily a developer, and built a large number of substantial terraced houses for letting in Duxbury Road, Turner Road and Thirlby Road.

About 1918-1920 he purchased a part of the Birstall Hall estate with the intention of developing the northern end of Curzon Avenue. He built a family home, "Whytegarth", on the corner of School Lane and Curzon Avenue, where he died in 1922. The firm also built two detached houses and a pair of substantial semis on Curzon Avenue. In 1928 Thomas Harry (1887-1952) moved into a new detached house designed by W. H. and H. G. Riley, built with hand-made bricks, and Swithland slates from the demolished Hall. It is interesting to note that the architect Cecil Ogden converted the stable block of the Hall into a sizeable house, and was a neighbour of the Duxburys. However, there is no evidence that he carried out professional work for them, although his son did so.

Henry Herbert and Sons

The firm was started about 1800, and developed by Henry Herbert (born 1842). At its peak it employed over 300 men, and was one of the largest building firms in the county. Henry Herbert built work designed by the Goddards and Stockdale Harrison, both commercial and housing projects. Buildings of particular significance included the Theatre Royal (1836) in Horsefair Street, by W. Parsons; St. James the Greater Church, Stoneygate (1899-1901) by Henry Langton Goddard; the Leicestershire Bank (now the Midland Bank), Granby Street, Leicester (1874), and the Leicestershire Club (1876-77) by Joseph Goddard; the Leicester School of Art (1896) by Everard Pick; and the Saracens Head (1904) in the Market Place, by Stockdale Harrison.

George Hewitt and Sons

George Hewitt (1834-1926) was a Leicester joiner and builder whose firm was responsible for significant housing developments. It was based at Ventnor House, 46 St. Peter's Road. Hewitt purchased land, cut the roads, and built housing between Avenue Road and Clarendon Park Road, and along Aylestone Road, Kimberley Road and London Road. According to his granddaughter, "he built a house a week for two years". George Hewitt was an active member of the Leicester Master Builders' Association, and was elected Vice-President at its inaugural meeting in February 1891. His three sons, George, Ernest and Charles, helped him to develop the business. The family home, built by him, was "The Glen" on the corner of Avenue Road and London Road.

J C Kellett and Son

John Cornelius Kellett founded the firm in 1830, which makes it one of the oldest building contractors in Leicester. Its original modest premises were in Asylum Street, in the Newarke area. John Henry (1859-1930) succeeded to the business about 1888, and in 1892 the firm moved to a three storey building at 40 Southgate Street. Next to the main building was a series of outbuildings including stables, store rooms for food and straw, and space for housing the cart and trap. He built his family home next to the works.

The firm carried out a wide range of projects including the erection and fitting out of many schools in Leicester. School furniture was accordingly manufactured in significant quantities. "To illustrate the size of the school furnishing operation, as many as 1,500 desks were being manufactured at one time", according to a history of the company by Lynne Kellett. Another notable scheme was the famous Victoria Coffee and Cocoa House in Granby Street, which was erected "for the advancement of temperance", and opened by the Duchess of Rutland in 1888.

By the end of the 19th century the erection of residential property, including three-storey villas, had been developed into a substantial part of the business. Unlike many local builders at this period, the firm did not carry out any speculative housing projects, but concentrated on detached houses and villas in the Stoneygate and Oadby areas. One of the firm's most prestigious buildings was Pares Bank, now the Westminster Bank, built in 1902 in St. Martins, to the design of the local architect S. Perkins Pick.

Stimpson and Rollston Limited

The firm was founded by Laban Stimpson (1848-1946) in 1885, when it was known as Stimpson and Wright. It later became Stimpson and Rollston and was developed by two of Laban's three sons, Israel and Benjamin - the third son, Albert was employed by Leicester City Council. Israel was the driving force. Among his many activities, he became President of the Midland Region Federation of Building Trades Employers in 1933. The company employed about 70 men and was originally based at Donnington Street and Cork Street. It finally moved to West Avenue, Wigston in 1955. In its early years it combined haulage, road building, joinery and housing. In 1913 its work even included a butcher's store on the corner of Mere Road and Egginton Street, clad in distinctive tiles.

Early in the 1920s the firm developed a significant area of land from the south side of Green Lane Road to Coleman Road, with the aid of a Government subsidy of £50 per house. After the Second World War, Israel's sons Frank, Ken and Tom successfully carried on the business until 1966, when Frank and Tom retired and it became part of Ellistown Pipes. The firm of F. Stimpson Ltd., formed by two sons of Thomas, is still trading at Staveley Road, Leicester and Chesterfield.

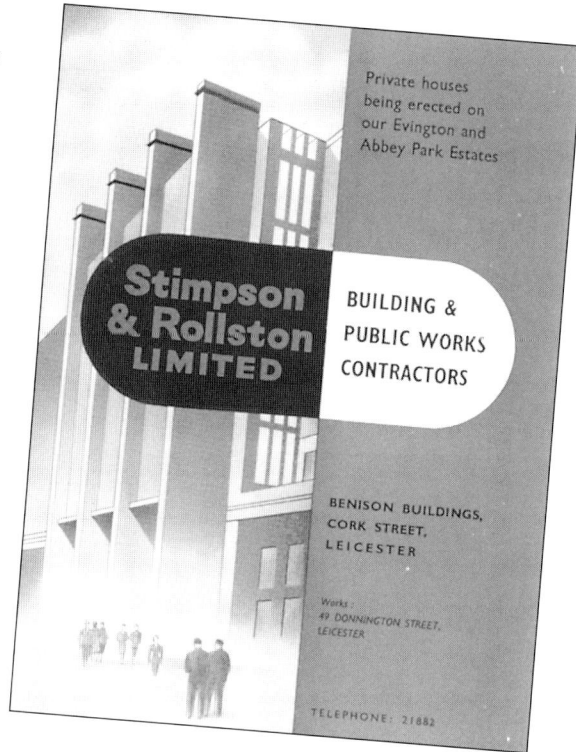

A 1950s advertisement for the well established firm of Stimpson and Rollston (Leicester City Council)

References

1. Briggs A., "A Social History of England", 1983, p 257.

CARISBROOKE (1878) LONDON ROAD STONEYGATE EAST
ARCHITECT: ISAAC BARRADALE
GRANT PITCHES '96

THE SUBURBS

"God is in the Details"[1]

In our survey of the middle class suburbs of Leicester, we have selected houses which, in our view, have that special quality which separates them from mere functional building. This is evident not only in their exterior appearance, but also in details such as newel posts, fireplaces and stained glass. This pursuit of detail was the basis for the richness of the domestic architecture of this period, but it has been difficult to obtain information on the specific work and names of the master joiners, woodcarvers, masons, roofers, and other highly-skilled craftsmen who implemented the architects' designs. These are the unsung heroes whose work enriched every facet of the architecture of this time.

References

1. Mies van der Rohe (1886-1969)

AYLESTONE ROAD

The setting

There is a limited amount of late 19th century domestic architecture in this area, about two miles (3KM) south east of the city centre, but it is of interest in the context of the middle class housing of the period. It is located overlooking the River Soar, by Goose Island on Aylestone Road, at a height of 60m O.D.

Significant houses

The most spectacular house - now demolished - was "Park Hill House", the home of the builder Orson Wright (now demolished). The site plan shows the nature of the setting to the house, with the tennis court an important element of the "Pleasure garden". Another example of a medium scale villa on the same road, dated about 1890, indicates the high quality of the brickwork and terracotta faience panels to the relieving arches to the windows. The contrasting use of red brick quoins to the white brickwork of the facades is employed in a number of houses in this area.

House on Aylestone Road (Helen Boynton)

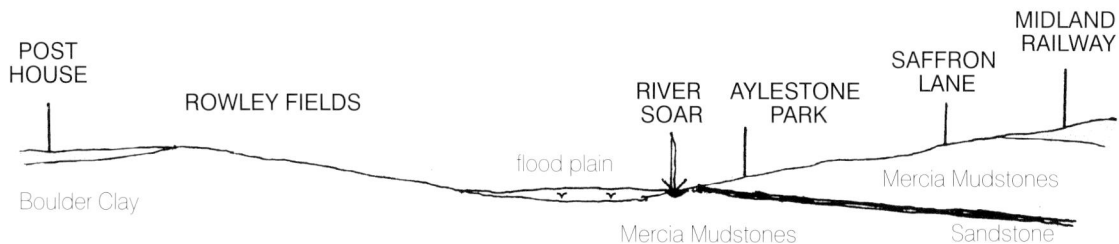

POST HOUSE — ROWLEY FIELDS — flood plain — RIVER SOAR — AYLESTONE PARK — SAFFRON LANE — MIDLAND RAILWAY

Boulder Clay — Mercia Mudstones — Mercia Mudstones — Sandstone

SECTION WNW-ESE ACROSS SOAR VALLEY

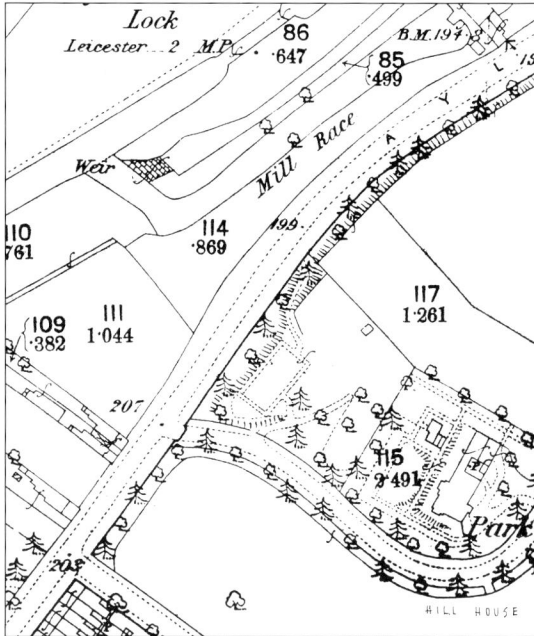

Site of Park Hill House (bottom right of map), off Aylestone Road

Lock
Leicester 2 M.P.
Weir
Mill Race
86 ·647
B.M.197
85 ·499
110 ·761
114 ·869
117 1·261
109 ·382
111 1·044
207
115 2·491
Park
HILL HOUSE

Park Hill House, now demolished. The photograph catches the mood of a family wedding morning. (Veronica Orson Wright)

BIRSTALL

The setting

Birstall is approximately two and a half miles (4KM) north east of Leicester. Its height above sea level is 50m O.D by the river, rising to 76m O.D. on the Golf Course. In the 19th century a large section of the working population was engaged in framework knitting, but the population grew only slowly - from 491 in 1851 to 611 in 1901. However, as communications improved with the opening of the Great Central railway in 1899, Birstall attracted new residents and registered a fourfold increase in population between 1921 and 1931, doubling again over the next 20 years.

The village grew up first around the church, and is situated on glacial gravels and boulder clay just west of the River Soar, which flows very close to the rising ground to the west. Later development took place along the junction of the boulder clays and gravels and the red marls, southwards along Birstall Lane, which is now known as Birstall Road. The houses on Birstall Road are built on fairly steep gradients, west of the flood plain of the river. It is an attractive aspect, with extensive sunny vistas facing east to Thurmaston across the valley of the Soar.

The development of Birstall is very interesting because of its relation to the topography and underlying geology. The sloping land with an eastern aspect, and firm boulder clay sites on the surface above the valley, were well utilised up to the 1930s. During the Edwardian period building took place along and near the main road to Loughborough, now the A6, on the upper slopes of the pleistocene sands and boulder clays, and on red Mercia Mudstone marls on the land of the Perseverance Land Company in the "V" between the A6 and Birstall Lane. Orange-brown sand of the glacial era can be seen in the banks on Leicester North Station, and on Birstall Golf Course, to the west.

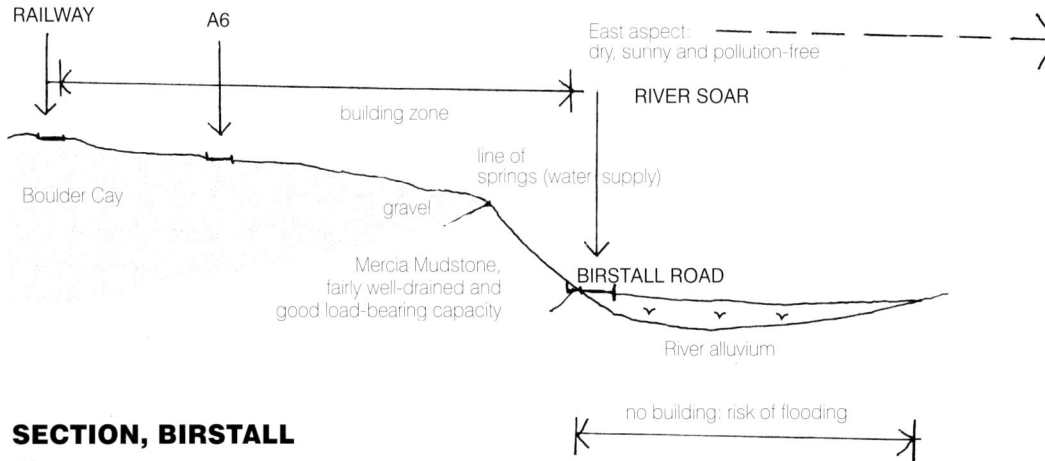

RAILWAY   A6

East aspect: dry, sunny and pollution-free

building zone

RIVER SOAR

line of springs (water supply)

Boulder Cay

gravel

Mercia Mudstone, fairly well-drained and good load-bearing capacity

BIRSTALL ROAD

River alluvium

no building: risk of flooding

SECTION, BIRSTALL

'BIRSTALL HOLT' : BIRSTALL LEICESTER
ARCHITECT. J. GODDARD. (1872)
GRANT PITCHES 95

Significant houses

Birstall's suburban development evolved from three significant estates founded and built by local businessmen: Birstall Hall, built in 1763 for Samuel Oliver, the last owner being Joseph Crisp Clarke; the Lawn Estate, home of the Pagets (1880-81); and the Goscote Hall Estate, home of Thomas Fielding Johnson Jnr. from 1895, built originally for James Jacques, a Leicester wool merchant, earlier in the century.

Architecturally, probably the most notable house in Birstall is "The Holt" (1880) on **Birstall Road**, designed by Joseph Goddard for W. H. Walker, a Leicester hosiery manufacturer. This is another interesting example of the "miniature estate", the house being set in about 15 acres. In a Warner, Sheppard and Wade sales brochure in 1923, it was described as "occupying a pleasant and retired position adjacent to the old-worlde Village of Birstall, about 200 feet above sea level, and commanding charming views over its own extensive and finely timbered grounds and across the intervening country to Billesdon Coplow... The property is in the Quorn Hunt and many of its meets are conveniently accessible. Birstall Golf Links are within a few minutes walk".

House in Curzon Avenue, Birstall (Helen Boynton)

Constructed in red brick with stone dressings and tiled roofs, its dominant features are the heavy gables to the main facades, tall chimneys and highly decorative details. They epitomise Goddard's style of this period, which was in essence English Revival.

The entrance lodge is in the same style, and is detailed with Goddard's flair for brick as ornament. Although described in 1923 as of moderate size", by today's standards it was luxurious, including a 12 feet square smoking room, billiard room and eight bedrooms as well as the usual drawing and dining rooms, plus a stable block with an 18 feet square heated garage. Within the grounds was "The Cottage" which was linked to "Tennis and Pleasure Lawns", and had its own servants' accommodation.

Overall, "The Holt" was a remarkable example of a late Victorian middle class gentleman's property. The former Holt estate stands on the west of Birstall Road, with infill houses between "The Lodge" and "The Cottage".

Birstall has a fairly complex and uneven quality of housing stock in relation to its size. However, there are some interesting smaller houses, including some Edwardian examples. On **Curzon Avenue**, for instance, there is a delightful rendered house with deep eaves and a "buttress" porch in the style of Voysey. On **Tempest Road** is an interesting house designed by Stockdale Harrison in 1923. It was brilliantly planned to respond to the constraints of the wedge-shaped site. In red and blue brickwork, its heavily-mullioned, angled bow windows give a powerful accent to the road facade.

In the early 1930s Shirley Harrison designed a group of houses, "Burley Houses", for retired people. The style was influenced by the Arts and Crafts movement, typified by the tall chimneys which are an important element in the composition.

EVINGTON

The setting

Evington is located approximately three miles east (5KM) of the centre of Leicester on a ridge of boulder clay and gravels at about 95m O.D.. Though incorporated into the City of Leicester in 1935, the central area still retains much of its "village" feel, and has been designated as a conservation area.

Two large estates came on the market in the early 1930s: Evington Hall, embracing an area of about 97 acres, and Evington House, formerly owned by Horace Pochin and covering around 32 acres. The latter was acquired by Leicester City Council for use as a park, and the house itself is now used as a recreation and training centre. The former Evington Hall, owned by John Faire, is now the Leicester Grammar School (Junior Department).

House in Linden Drive (Helen Boynton)

Significant houses

An attempt to develop a low-density estate in Evington for Leicester's businessmen in the earlier 20th century was thwarted by the advent of the First World War. The Uplands estate was to be developed by Clare and Simons, a Leicester firm of architects and surveyors. In fact only one house was built -"Uplands" itself, on the corner of **Spencefield Lane** and **Uppingham Road**, which is still in excellent condition today. It was designed using soft red brickwork for the "base" and chimney stacks, contrasting with the white-rendered walls. It features a Venetian and double-height window with stained glass on the road facade.

There are also two notable buildings in **Linden Drive**, named like the nearby **Hawthorne Drive** after the types of trees planted there. One is an unusual but interesting house (c.1912) with a domed leaded roof capping the entrance. A more conventional house on the same road has a deep curved gable as a central feature to the main facade, and an elegant entrance porch featuring Doric columns. It was designed for his own occupation by William Wells, partner of Arthur Wakerley.

The name of the architect Arthur Wakerley (1862-1931) is rightly remembered for his pioneering work in developing the industrial suburb of North Evington. Wakerley also designed a limited number of detached houses, including "Crown Hill House" (1901-2) in **Gwendolen Road**, a large gabled one-bay cube shaped building.

William Wells' house in Linden Drive (above), and (right) detail of window in Hawthorne Drive (Helen Boynton)

GREAT GLEN

The setting

Great Glen is approximately six miles (9KM) south east of the centre of Leicester. The area varies in height from 98m O.D. at the river to 128m at Great Glen Manor. The River Sence cuts through the boulder clay into the Lower Lias shales, although these are rarely exposed. The upper slopes are covered with boulder clay, and the river valley has an alluvium flood plain. The architectural character of the centre of Great Glen is largely unspoilt as it has been classified as a Conservation Area.

Significant houses

Two houses, built in the same year but very different in their scale of accommodation and architectural style, represent two facets of Edwardian social status. "Glen Lodge" (1906), a medium size villa, was designed for the leather merchant Mr J. H. Brown, by the architect Lawton Brown. Built in red brickwork with stone lintels, mullioned windows and a slate roof, it is a handsome, informally planned building. The entrance facade is asymmetrical, with its two-storey entrance wing capped by a curved parapet surmounted with stone balls. The house and garden are linked by a wide terrace, which gives an excellent threshold to the lawned garden. The external quality of the house is characterised by the superb brick work with diaper patterning to the chimney stacks.

"The Manor" (1906-7 - now Stoneygate School, Junior Department), was designed by one of Leicester's most famous architects, Joseph Goddard. The house and its estate of over 50 acres indicates the status of its first owner, Robert W. Kaye, J.P., who still owned it in the 1930s. It was set in an idyllic landscape, "standing well removed from the main London Road at an elevation of over 400 feet above sea level, with principal aspects and extensive views over fine pastoral countryside to the South and West". (Warner Sheppard and Wade sales catalogue, 9 July 1935). Like similar properties of this scale, it was protected by an entrance lodge, one of four "excellent Lodges and Cottages for Servants".

The gardens adjacent to the house were typical of the Edwardian gardens of the wealthy, geared to pleasure with "utmost seclusion". On the main south front they included "Spacious Double Tennis Lawn to accommodate Four Courts"; and on the northern side, a formal rose garden designed in rectangular beds with

THE WOODLANDS
AND GLEN LODGE

GREAT GLEN

River Sence

Lower Lias clays

Lower Lias clays

Boulder Clay and gravels

SECTION NE-SW, GREAT GLEN

North Elevation.

**Glen Lodge,
with window
detail below
(Helen Boynton)**

Details of interiors, The Manor (Helen Boynton)

clipped box borders, sheltered by a tall yew hedge. The design of the house poses some interesting questions for the architectural historian, particularly the main entrance frontage. Joseph Goddard has incorporated an unusual detail into the gable. It is basically a chequerboard pattern using napped-flint panels and stonework - an uncharacteristic use of material for the Leicester area. A similar detail was included five years earlier in the first phase of "Marshcourt" in Hampshire, which was designed by the nationally famous architect, Edwin Lutyens. His work was always published in Country Life by his patron Edward Hudson, and it is a distinct possibility that Goddard was influenced by this house.

The accommodation included a "charming Lounge Hall (approx. 24 x 17 feet), Morning Room or Study (14 feet square) and a handsome Drawing or Music Room (31 x 20 feet)". In the north western wing was a billiard room and spacious library. There were seven large scale bedrooms, and day and night nurseries on the second floor. The servants' quarters on the top floor consisted of "four good Maids' Bedrooms".

The overriding impression of the interior of the house is one of quality of detail. In the principal rooms are examples of the joiner's and woodcarver's art. Surely this is the essence of the interior of this period - demonstrated in the pursuit of exquisite quality by craftsmen who took tremendous pride in their work. Particularly striking features are the oak staircase with its "barleysugar" balustrade, and the panelling and friezes in oak in the library with the rams' heads accentuating the pilasters.

KIRBY FIELDS
(KIRBY MUXLOE)

The setting

Kirby Muxloe is located approximately three miles (5KM) due west of Leicester. It includes the area known as Kirby Fields, which was developed on a gentle west facing slope of land between Kirby Muxloe village and the A47 Hinckley Road. It is covered with boulder clays and gravels at about 91m O.D.. These rocks pass downwards into the red marls of the Mercia Mudstones on the lower slopes nearer the brook, the boundary between Kirby Fields and Kirby Muxloe village. The ground at Kirby Fields provided firm, well-drained sites for building purposes, and its south westerly aspects would be relatively sunny. Over the years this area has had more trees planted, making it relatively shady.

A fundamental change to the area evolved with the purchase of Kirby Fields in 1877 by Matthew Brady, a Leicester shoe manufacturer. He divided the 77 acre estate into 41 building plots which he offered for sale. The potential of the area was also seen by another

Detail of door handle, The Glen (Helen Boyton)

footwear manufacturer, Sir Edward Wood, who bought a number of plots to develop himself. Development took place along four primary roads - Hastings Road, Forest Drive, Stamford Road and Charnwood Road - from the north of the estate to the southern edge which was bounded by the Midland Railway line between Leicester and Burton-on-Trent.

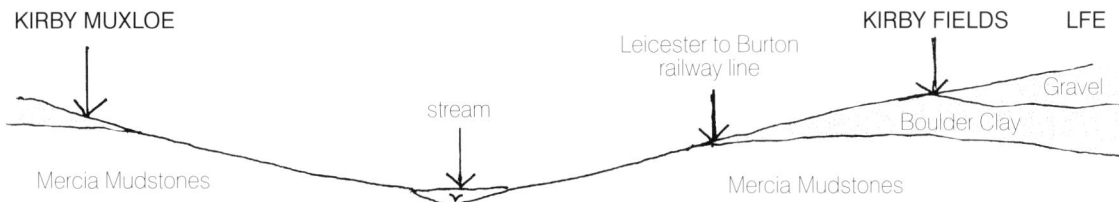

KIRBY MUXLOE

stream

Leicester to Burton
railway line

KIRBY FIELDS   LFE

Gravel

Boulder Clay

Mercia Mudstones

Mercia Mudstones

SECTION NW-SE, KIRBY MUXLOE AND KIRBY FIELDS

Significant houses

The area was largely developed on sites of about two acres, on which were located houses designed by some of Leicester's most fashionable architects, including G. Lawton Brown who designed his own family home here. In the late 19th century Kirby Fields matched Stoneygate and Oadby in popularity among the middle classes, offering the desired combination of space, privacy and high quality housing, and having a similar social structure. Its residents included a solicitor and doctors as well as industrialists - but unlike either Stoneygate or Oadby, it had its own railway station, opened in 1859.

Kirby Fields epitomised a style of living based on wealth and a sense of class separation, protected from the outside world by medium-scale gardens. According to a survey of historically significant houses and their occupants by Kirby Muxloe Women's Institute: "Every Easter the nine-hole golf course was taken over for a mixed-golf match, and the first week in August brought the Invitation Tennis Tournament between Kirby Muxloe and Desford, played on the many tennis courts of the Kirby Fields houses". It is also interesting to note that the idyllic social life was not limited to the summer months, and "winter evenings were occupied by rehearsals for the Pierrots, a concert party started by Major H. L. Midgley of Stamford House".

Five houses typify the range of late Victorian and early Edwardian properties in this area. "The Glen" (1890), owned by James Turner, the well-known leather merchant, was built in a pale buff brick with red brick

Forest Lodge and Stamford House (Helen Boynton)

Moel Llys
(Helen Boynton)

quoins and lintels. It has a dominant slate roof, with tall multi-faceted chimneys. The garden facade is most attractive, with its asymmetric large gable. An exquisite internal detail is the metal push-plate and door handle.

"Stamford House" and "Forest House" (1895) are a pair of large three-storey semi-detached houses built for William Harding, a coal merchant. The ground and first floors are in brickwork, with contrasting quoins and diaperwork used to accent the bedroom windows. The top floor walls are rendered with diamond features on the deep gables. The entrance porch with its coloured glass fanlight and richly moulded wood mullions gives a feeling of affluence.

"Moel Llys" (1902) was built for William Wheeler Kendall, an umbrella manufacturer of Leicester. It was probably designed by the local architect Lawton Brown. Kendall was a very successful businessman, and by the time he died in 1910 he owned 37 shops as well as a new factory in Belvoir Street, Leicester. It is a dramatic building, and is typically eclectic with a mixture of styles: a "Queen Anne" gabled wing on the entrance facade, a corner turret on the return elevation, and large deep gables on both. The entrance detail, however is more restrained, and is an elegant study of stonework using Ionic pilasters.

"The Barncroft" (1904) was built for Thomas Hollis, of the timber firm, Hollis Brothers. The interiors reflect the owner's business background, and are characterised by the use of exotic and beautifully detailed timbers. A particularly striking feature is the staircase and generous upper landing in beech strip, with exotic woods used as inlays in the form of a star. The main entrance in

**Detail of landing floor, The Barncroft
(Helen Boynton)**

stonework is well-detailed, and incorporates beautifully carved Ionic pilasters.

One of the architects who lived latterly at Kirby Fields was Ralph Waldo Bedingfield. He designed two houses, "Ringwood" - which he occupied himself and "White Cottage", on adjacent plots in the late 1920s. Both had white rough cast walls and heavy roof forms, and indicate the continuing influence of C. F. A. Voysey.

LEICESTER FRITH AND GLENFIELD FRITH

The setting

Leicester Frith and Glenfield Frith are between two and two and a half miles (3-4KM) west of the centre of Leicester. The Glenfield Frith estate lay on the south side of the A50 Glenfield Road.

Significant houses

Set back from Glenfield Road, in the grounds of Glenfield General Hospital, is an imposing house designed by William Keay and known locally as "Leicester Frith". It was built in 1870 of Charnian diorite, probably from Markfield, with sandstones of Millstone Grit age, some showing bedding features as mullions, quoins, lintels and transoms.

Sale brochure photograph of Glenfield Frith, now demolished

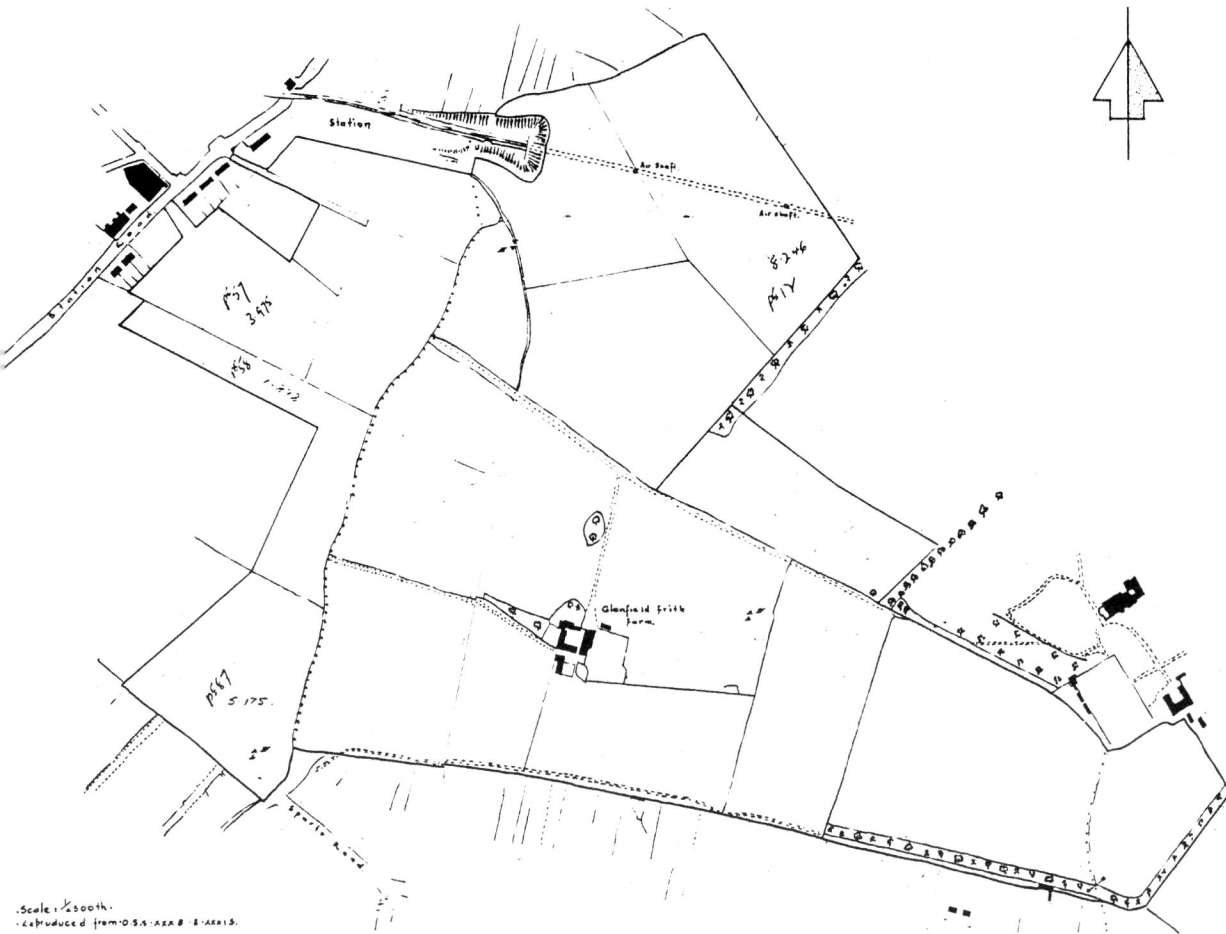

Station

Air Shaft

Air Shaft

Glenfield Frith Farm

.Scale : 1/2500th.
.Reproduced from .O.S.S .A.X.A.B .S .A.X.A.S.

· S I T E · P L A N · G L E N F I E L D · F R I T H · E S T A T E ·

·George ·Culverley ·&· Sons (Contractors) Ltd·
·Building · & · Civil · Engineering · Contractors·
·Errington · Valley · Road ·
· Leicester ·

Leicester Frith with detail of
Charnian diorite walling with
gargoyle; and (on facing page)
detail of newel post and entrance
(Helen Boynton)

It stands on the site of an earlier house known as "Markham's Close", possibly of Tudor origin, with a chapel 100 yards to the west. The present house was built in 1870 for Mr Swift-Taylor, J.P., cotton thread manufacturer, whose factory was in Mansfield Street. On his death it served in turn as a home for "Genteel Ladies", and for soldiers suffering from shell shock during the First World War. After the war it was purchased by the Borough Council and became the Leicester Female Mental Deficiency Home. The most dramatic feature of the interior is the large entrance hall,

which includes an open-well staircase with elaborately carved oak newel posts lit by a four-light window.

The Glenfield Frith estate, which lay on the south side of the A50, was put up for sale in the 1940s. It extended to the south and south west and belonged to Samuel Faire J.P., D.L., Managing Director of Faire Brothers. Much of the land was later sold for housing development – it includes Faire Road – and "Glenfield Frith Hall" itself was demolished after the Second World War. It was built in Elizabethan style with stone mullioned windows and leaded-lights.

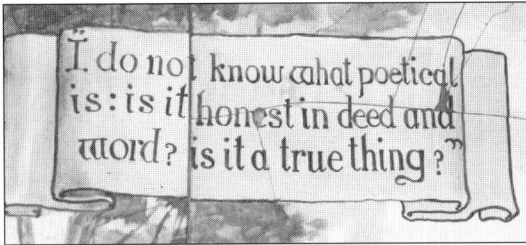
Wall tiling, The Ferns (Helen Boynton)

LOUGHBOROUGH ROAD
(Conservation Area)

The setting

The area between between Windsor Avenue and Rowsley Street, now a Conservation Area, developed in the late 19th century on the margin of the glacial sands and gravels and red marls on the eastern side of the River Soar flood plain. Sandy soil is still found in some of the gardens between Loughborough Road and Melton Road. The junction of the glacial deposits and red marls would probably have been marked by a spring-line.

Loughborough Road was a suitable area for building, at a convenient distance from the town centre. The west facing aspect would be particularly pleasant in the summer, but the land was relatively low (around 50m) and prone to mist and fog from the nearby river. Higher sites would have been found during the late Edwardian period as building developed outwards from the inner areas of the city. The area is comparable in some degree in building development, geology and topography with the Aylestone Road near to Grace Road.

Significant houses

The area of initial development was on the eastern edge of the road, where large detached and semi-detached villas were built on generous plots which were subsequently landscaped. In the late 1880s **Shaftesbury Avenue** was speculatively developed for the growing numbers of professional people. However,

as the suburb of Stoneygate became fashionable, the Loughborough Road area slowly began to decline. It includes a diverse range of examples of Victorian domestic architecture, especially houses of the English Vernacular Revival style. These feature tile-hanging to the large scale bay windows, which are capped by deep projecting half-timbered gables.

Three buildings demonstrate either exceptional architectural quality or remarkable interior features of this period. "The Ferns", built in 1885 and occupied for some time by Dr Noble, formerly of Danett's Hall, was planned to provide appropriate accommodation for the middle class life-style of the time. It included a well-

appointed billiard room, large fireplaces, and a bathroom with exquisite tiles. The generous entrance hall had as its focus a spectacular sculpture which could have graced the interior of a large country house.

A second house, built in 1865, includes an interior with a mahogany-framed mirror, incorporating elaborately carved brackets to the cornice in the form of children's heads.

Within the wide range of architectural styles of the semi-detached villas on Loughborough Road there are also fine examples of the "Queen Anne" curved gables. These give further variety and interest to the road.

OADBY

The setting

Oadby is approximately three and a half miles (6KM) south east of Leicester. In 1881 it had a population of 1,731, rising to 3,279 in 1921. The main Leicester-London Road passed through the village, and although it had no railway station, its growth was encouraged after 1874 by the advent of horse-drawn trams, with termini at the city boundary and the Black Dog in Oadby. In 1904 the electric tram opened up London Road, and this encouraged further development. The wealthy, of course, travelled by personal transport: horse-drawn carriage, and later motor carriages.

The same ridge on which the A6 London Road runs also extends out along Knighton Grange Road on to Manor Road and beyond. As the ground rises up from the city boundary on the A6, the Washbrook is crossed near the large roundabout - the stream is now underground - and the Lower Lias clays form the underlying geology here, although not exposed. The glacial gravels are crossed near the ASDA store, causing the increase in the gradient, and then the road continues into the county on the boulder clays. Oadby is about 80m O.D. above sea level at the city boundary, rising to approximately 90m O.D. at the Hermitage Hotel.

There was one main landowner, the Powys-Keck estate, whose Oadby lands were sold off and developed over a period of around 20 years from the turn of the century. Glebe Road was laid down in 1902, and the first houses to be built in the area were "Nether Close" (now "Hastings House") and "One Oak" (now "Kent") in that year. Development continued out from the city boundary, and Knighton Rise was developed from the eastern end of Stoughton Drive South, westwards to the city boundary. Later developments included the Leicestershire Golf Club (1913) and parts of Manor Road in 1920. The areas of Oadby examined here are characterised by low density housing, wide roads and pavements and a generally tranquil ambience. A number of roads are tree-lined, and the sites vary in area from a minimum of half an acre in Knighton Rise, to up to four acres in Stoughton Drive South.

House in Knighton Rise c.1912 (Helen Boynton)

Significant houses

On **Knighton Rise** there are several large Edwardian villas, some of which have been listed. H. C. Sturgess-Wells of the Sturwell Leather Co. was a key figure in the development of Knighton Rise, after building "The Poplars" in 1906 for his own occupation. Concerned by the lack of public amenities in the area, he became active on the Parish Council and helped to secure a mains drainage system, and improved street lighting in the village. Higher grade public services were expected to attract local businessmen from Leicester, and increase rateable values.

There are two particularly fine examples of Edwardian houses on Knighton Rise. One was designed in 1906 by the architect A. Hall of 8 St. Martins Leicester, for Mr Frank Snowden, a gentlemen's outfitter and tailor with premises on the corner of Charles Street and Humberstone Gate. It features large semi-circular bays with curved glass. The other was one of the last houses built before the outbreak of the First World War. It is an exciting example of the Arts and Crafts idiom, featuring a series of dramatic gables with Swiss-style deep eaves, and elaborate hand-carved bargeboards. A further feature is the tile-hanging to the gables and first floors.

Knighton Grange Road was originally a farm road connecting Knighton Grange to London Road at the end of the 19th century. During the early 20th century Manor Road was laid down eastwards, and Stoughton Drive South northwards. The southern portion of Knighton Grange Road was renamed Stoughton Drive South. This area is part of the Hill Top Conservation Area, and includes a number of listed (Grade 2) houses.

Glebe Road originally fell within the town boundary, but later alterations placed it in the county. The original plans for the road were drawn up in 1902, and a number of houses date from 1903-7.

GLEBE HOUSE : OADBY (c 1907)
ARCHITECT R.W. BEDINGFIELD (1872 - 1940)

There are several Edwardian houses which have listed status including the first to be built, "Glebe Mount" (1903), for Marshall Pearson, a partner in the British United Shoe Machinery Company on Belgrave Road.

Two other houses of a more distinctive quality deserve detailed comment. The first, called "Cluanbeag" (meaning "little field") was designed in 1907 by one of Leicester's most talented architects of the period, Walter Bedingfield. His client was Duncan Henderson, a shoe manufacturer. It is currently called "Glebe House".

Its features indicate that the architect was influenced by the work of C. F. A. Voysey: the large bracketed eaves are one clear example. The interiors also reflect his influence. The beautiful stained glass in the billiard room, for instance, is based on his tulip motif.

The second house, "The Knoll" (1907), was built for William Winterton, a local brick manufacturer, and designed by Stockdale and Shirley Harrison in the Elizabethan Revival style. It is constructed of special hand-made Tudor bricks, and has a Swithland slate roof. A feature of the brickwork is the incorporation of diaper patterns. The entrance facade is dominated by the tall diagonal-based chimneys used on a number of the Stockdale Harrison houses of this period. The entrance hall emphasises the status of the owners, with an elaborate fully-beamed ceiling, floor to ceiling wood panelling, and a low-relief white frieze depicting the seven Graces. The main planting of the gardens dates from 1910.

On **Stoughton Drive North**, "Middlemeade" (1904 - now Beaumont Hall) is one of the most spectacular houses in this area, designed by Stockdale and Shirley Harrison for the hosiery manufacturer F. S. Brice at a cost of around £18,000. It is a classic example of the "miniature estate", with extensive gardens started in 1905 and completed in 1920. Helen Boynton notes in her booklet "Prospect of Oadby" (1993) that Mr Brice employed ten gardeners - five for the greenhouses, and five for outside work.

The architects were well known for their Elizabethan Revival style, one of the products of the Arts and Crafts Movement. "Middlemeade" epitomised this style, with dominant gables, mullioned windows, tall elaborately moulded chimneys, and black and white half-timbering to the principal facades. Built in brick with diaper designs, it is an excellent example of brick-detailing.

The entrance hall creates a sense of status, achieved by a large scale open well or "open newel" staircase, "communicating ideas of prestige and status as well as style".

"Nether Close" (1902 - now "Hastings House") was also designed by Stockdale and Shirley Harrison, for the hosiery manufacturer W. H. Stevens. It is situated on an extensive site sloping down to London Road. The architects sensitively created large terraces which provided a generous social context to the house. The ruins of Ragdale Hall, captured in a pencil sketch by Shirley Harrison in 1895, were probably the inspiration for this magnificent building, with its black and white timbered elevations and dominant two-storey projecting bays in brick with stone dressings. The 17th century flavour is emphasised by the tall faceted chimneys.

Manor Road was laid down from the western end early this century. "The Coppice" (c.1907 - DMU) is one of its most significant houses, designed by Everard and Pick and located on the corner of Manor Road and Stoughton Drive South, in a garden of about two acres. The twin gables are a key feature of the main facade. It is interesting in that the gables are linked, and are boarded not tiled. This is a clear reference to "Standen" (1891), an important house designed by Philip Webb (1831-1915) an early Arts and Crafts architect, which also influenced the work of Lutyens at "Homewood"

Detail of newel post, The Coppice, Oadby (Helen Boynton)

(1901). The interiors are modest in their detail, as typified by the newel post with its simple capping and Voysey hearts - a far cry from the luxury of "Nether Close".

"Aigburth", now a Methodist Home for the Aged, is a hybrid design, and is difficult to date without clear evidence. The porch is dated 1907, but the brickwork is later - probably mid 1920s. It was built for J. G. Pickard, Chairman of the Governors of Leicester Infirmary, whose religious beliefs were reflected in the symbolism of the stained-glass windows with their proverbs.

"Sorrento" (1906 - now "Shirley House") was built for the footwear manufacturer Robert Hyslop, and later occupied by Mr A. Lorrimer, Managing Director of Pool Lorrimer and Tabberer. The architect has not been identified, but it is an interesting example of a modified Arts and Crafts style. The dominant external feature of this house are the large scale deeply projected gables to the main facades. These have beautifully carved barge boards. Central to the gables are small elliptical windows in elaborately carved stone surrounds. The influence of Shaw is seen in the well-detailed tile-hanging to the gables and the whole first floor.

"The Beeches" (1920) was one of the later houses designed by Stockdale and Shirley Harrison to an L-shaped plan. It is Neo-Georgian, popular in the 1920s and early 30s. Built in brick from Tring, it features Georgian-style vertical-sliding sash windows. The main characteristic is the uniform pattern of windows enriched with horizontal-banded brickwork. The dining room is beautifully detailed with restrained classical pilasters, and built-in display cabinets.

Meadowcourt Road was laid down in 1910 by the architects A. E. and T. Sawday. Houses on the even-numbered side of the road were mainly built before the odd-numbered ones. Most of the houses were built on sites of around a quarter of an acre, either by the Sawdays or by the architect Frank Jones. Covenants still exist among the trustees of the estate and can be upheld in law. In 1910 these stated that any house built on the corner of Meadowcourt Road and London Road must not cost less than £1,500! An interesting feature of this development is the inclusion of a number of "Y" plan houses, influenced by the seminal building of Edward S. Prior (1852-1932) at Exmouth in Devon, "Priors Barn" (1897). This was the prototype for a number of houses developed by regional architects for Leicester businessmen.

"The Hermitage" (1901 - currently a hotel), opposite St. Peter's church, was designed by Goddard and Catlow. One of the most spectacular Edwardian houses outside the Manor Road area, it was a small residential estate with around six acres of "Beautiful Pleasure Grounds", and a "small grazing holding" of around 42 acres with five

NETHER CLOSE' (1902) (HASTINGS HOUSE) OADBY
ARCHITECT : STOCKDALE HARRISON

Detail of stained glass panels, Aigburth, Oadby (Helen Boynton)

cottages. It was designed for the hosiery manufacturer T. G. Hirst in a modified Elizabethan Revival style, in red brick with stone dressings and timber work. The main features are the gables on both the garden and street frontages. Stone mullioned windows with leaded light casements increase the manorial look. Like many of Leicester's larger houses of this period, it was roofed in graduated Swithland slate.

The accommodation reflected the social mores of the middle class at this time. It included the usual "Suite of Entertaining Rooms": drawing, dining, smoking and billiards rooms. There were four double and one single bedrooms, and on the top floor a "capital suite of rooms for two maids". Typical also of this scale of estate in Leicestershire was a hunting stable block comprising four loose boxes, harness and cleating rooms.

The Framework Knitters' Homes (1906) and the Corah Memorial Homes (1924-1926) on **Stoughton Road** were both designed in the Arts and Crafts tradition, in brick with gabled-roofs and tile-hanging. The former includes a hall, immaculately detailed, and a classically inspired mahogany wall panel of names of members of the Worshipful Company of Framework Knitters.

The Corah Almshouses were built as a memorial to Leslie Corah, son of the local hosiery manufacturer, who was killed in the First World War in 1918.

ROTHLEY (PLAIN)

The setting

Rothley Plain is approximately six miles (9 KM) north north west of Leicester, and was accessible to the town by means of the Great Central Railway. The height of the area is 70m O.D.

Significant houses

The most interesting house (1901) is located on **The Ridgeway**, and was owned at one time by the footwear manufacturer Edward Wood. Its main architectural features are the dominant roof with varied size dormers, dentils, and the pedimented main entrance.

Also on The Ridgeway is "Fairfield", with an Arts and Crafts flavour, dated 1901. The details include large diagonal-grouped brick chimney stacks, and deep projecting double gables. "Paigles" (1902), the third house of interest, is also located on The Ridgeway, and was designed by Stockdale Harrison.

House on The Ridgeway (Helen Boynton)

FAIRFIELD' (1901) ROTHLEY LEICS

GRANT PITCHES '96

STONEYGATE
(Conservation Area)

The setting

Stoneygate was one of the most sought after suburbs of Leicester. It lies around a mile and a half south east (2KM) of the city centre, and stretches from Victoria Park in the north to the city boundary with Oadby to the south. It is divided into two by London Road, which runs approximately down the centre of a fairly narrow ridge of boulder clay and gravels, from which the land slopes gently away on both sides. The slope on the east side is slightly steeper than that on the west side, but this ridge of land with firm well-drained boulder clays and gravels provided ideal sites for building. The height of the area is around 80m O.D..

The land on the east side of London Road was largely owned by the Powys-Keck estate. The pattern of ownership was more complex on the western side, but here the significant landowners included Wallis Goddard (1851-1927), who founded an international business based on silver plate powder, and the Craddocks of Knighton. The many tree-lined streets are one of Stoneygate's environmental attractions. The large scale

CARIS BROOKE (1878) LONDON ROAD STONEY GATE EAST
ARCHITECT : ISAAC BARRADALE

villas can be seen through and against this green backcloth, and together create an ambience of serenity.

Compared to the areas of Oadby which are included in its Conservation Areas, Stoneygate has generally a higher density of housing. In East Stoneygate it is characterised by a mixture of terraced three storey brick villas of the late Victorian period, which often feature stained glass porches and entrance halls; and in the western sector by larger detached houses in gardens of two to four acres.

SECTION NW-SE, STONEYGATE – KNIGHTON – OADBY

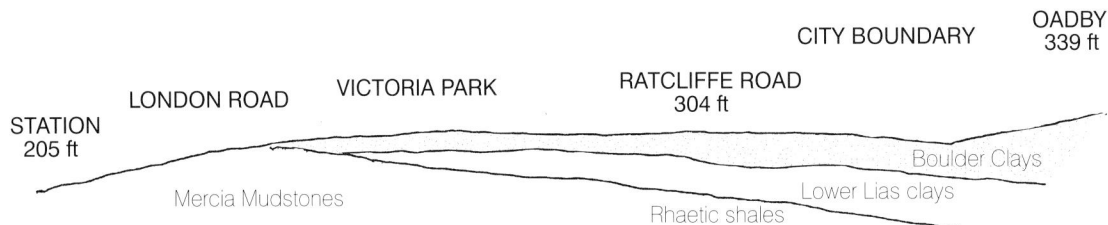

CITY BOUNDARY

OADBY
339 ft

RATCLIFFE ROAD
304 ft

LONDON ROAD

VICTORIA PARK

STATION
205 ft

Mercia Mudstones

Boulder Clays

Lower Lias clays

Rhaetic shales

Stoneygate East

Isaac Barradale, one of the most talented of Leicester's architects, designed two villas of dramatic quality on **Stanley Road** in 1878, for two sisters who wished to live near each other but not together. The project was financed by their father. Barradale was influenced by the Arts and Crafts movement, and his domestic work is characterised by large projecting timbered gables, open balconies, and black and white half-timbering. "Carisbrooke", one of these villas (currently used by a dental practice), is an excellent example of his panache in "modelling" facades, combining superb detailing of elements.

St. John's Road includes a striking example of late Victorian semi-detached villas. Built about 1890, their twin gables are an essay in black and white half-timbering.

In many ways, tree-lined **Stoneygate Road** typifies the mood of Stoneygate East in its quality of houses of this period and their setting. It includes the classic three-storey late Victorian terraced villas designed by Isaac Barradale. "Stoneleigh" (c.1870 - now converted into flats) is atypical of this area, having a large site of approximately 5.75 acres. A reflection of the wealth of the original owner was the use of very expensive building materials, including Charnian diorites, possibly supplied from Markfield.

Holmfield Road was laid down about 1910, and includes an interesting house dated 1912 (architect unknown) typical of the late Edwardian villas of this area.

Built in warm red brickwork with banded stone string courses, its symmetrical facade to the road embodies the middle class values of stability and love of quality. Its key features are the twin gables with associated large bowed windows, linking the ground and first floors.

The garden elevation incorporates a decorative timber verandah with shallow lintels framing views to the romantic garden. In the interior, the hall has a fine richly patterned mosaic floor, but the principal element which gives particular richness to its interior is the double height stained glass window. This is a striking example of the glassmaker's art

Just inside the city boundary, **Westminster Road** includes a mixed group of semi-detached houses, some of which are three-storey late Edwardian in vintage. Some of the architects and builders were no doubt influenced by C. F. A. Voysey, as white roughcast walls are the dominant feature with contrasting tiled roofs. One semi-detached house includes a small, charming Voyseyesque projected two-storey stub wing, with exaggerated full height buttresses. The architect Norman Read designed a number of properties in this area.

Stoneleigh, Stoneygate Road (above) and Allandale (below and right) both pictured in sale brochures.

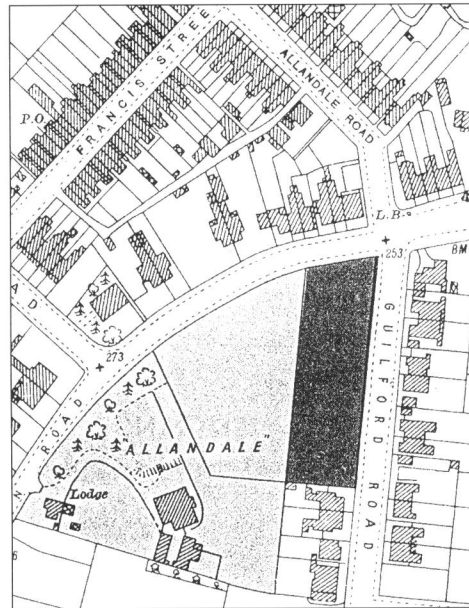

Allandale Road was a typical middle class residential road, whose occupants included managers, an architect and a schoolmaster. The original estate which gave the area its name was known as "Allandale", and was sold at an auction in 1938. It covered "3 acres 0 Roods 16 Perches or thereabouts", stretching from Stoughton Road to Guilford Road to the east.

"Allandale" was a strange hybrid Regency, "of Distinctive Elevation of Old Fashioned type, occupying a pleasantly retired situation" The accommodation was typical of this size of villa, with "four Reception Rooms, five Principal and Secondary bedrooms, reached from a Galleried Landing". Its status was reinforced by a large entrance lodge for the servants, and its privacy and security was achieved by "well matured Timber Trees, the front being well protected by a Deep Spinney Belt". The gardens included the ubiquitous sunken tennis lawn, kitchen gardens, orchard and small paddock.

London Road is bordered by a rich range of houses of the late Victorian and Edwardian periods. Unfortunately, like other suburbs in Leicester, it suffered from a wave of demolitions in the 1960's and 70s. However, it still includes the work of some of Leicester's famous architects of this time, among them Joseph Goddard and Stockdale Harrison.

One of the Gothic designs by Joseph Goddard, formerly St. Francis nursing home, and currently a residential nursing home, was designed in 1879 and features some beautiful stained glass designs of birds. Goddard's High Victorian work on London Road also includes "Brookfield" (1876-78), currently Charles Frears Campus of De Montfort University.

Detail of stained glass in the former St. Francis nursing home on London Road. (Helen Boynton)

Stoneygate West (Conservation Area)

Stoneygate West includes the elite domestic architecture of what is probably Leicester's most prestigious Victorian suburb. It has a remarkable range of spectacular houses, some of which were designed by Leicester's famous trio of architects: Joseph Goddard, Isaac Barradale and Stockdale Harrison and Son.

Probably the most famous house in **Knighton Park Road** is "The Hawthorns", the home of Wilmot Pilsbury, first Principal of the Leicester School of Art. It was built in 1882 and designed by Isaac Barradale. Pilsbury had a top-lit studio on the top floor of the house, and it has a facade to the road of great charm which includes intricate incised plasterwork panels, and the wyvern of the town arms on the roof.

A wide range of architects designed houses on Springfield Road, from R. W. Bedingfield, Redfern and Sawday, Stockdale Harrison & Son, to Arthur Wakerley. They include two particularly fine examples of late Victorian villas. "Abingdon House" (1892), designed by Stockdale Harrison and Son, is a powerful evocation of middle class status. Three-storeyed, double-bayed, with a beautifully detailed semi-circular arched entrance and stained glass fanlight, it declares the wealth of its owners. The red-brick asymmetrical facade includes a third storey with bracketed projecting gable, counter-poised by a five-sided hipped roof clad at this level with vertical tiling. The heavy mullioned bays are also linked with similar tiling.

The quality of the external and internal details is remarkable. Even the smallest utilitarian features are carefully handled - the dated rainwater head is an excellent example. The interior staircases, always a measure of status, are particularly fine: the main mahogany stair with its elaborate stepped balusters and carved strings, and the servants' pine stair with its turned newel capping and panel of carved oak leaves.

Rainwater heads, Springfield Road; and bell push, Church House, Stoneygate Avenue (Helen Boynton)

COAL HOUSE

LAVATORY

SCULLERY

KITCHEN
11'0" X 7'0"

CONSERVATORY

DN

GARDEN

TRIPLE GABLES

BREAKFAST ROOM
11'0" X 11'0"

NORTH ELEVATION TO ROAD

S

N

TWO STOREY
COACH HOUSE

CONSERVATORY

LOBBY

LARDER

DOWN TO
CELLAR

BACK
RECEPTION RM
16'0" X 13'0"

DELF RAIL

UP

HALL

FRONT
RECEPTION
18'0" X 15'0"

ROAD

BLOCK PLAN

ENTRANCE

GROUND FLOOR PLAN

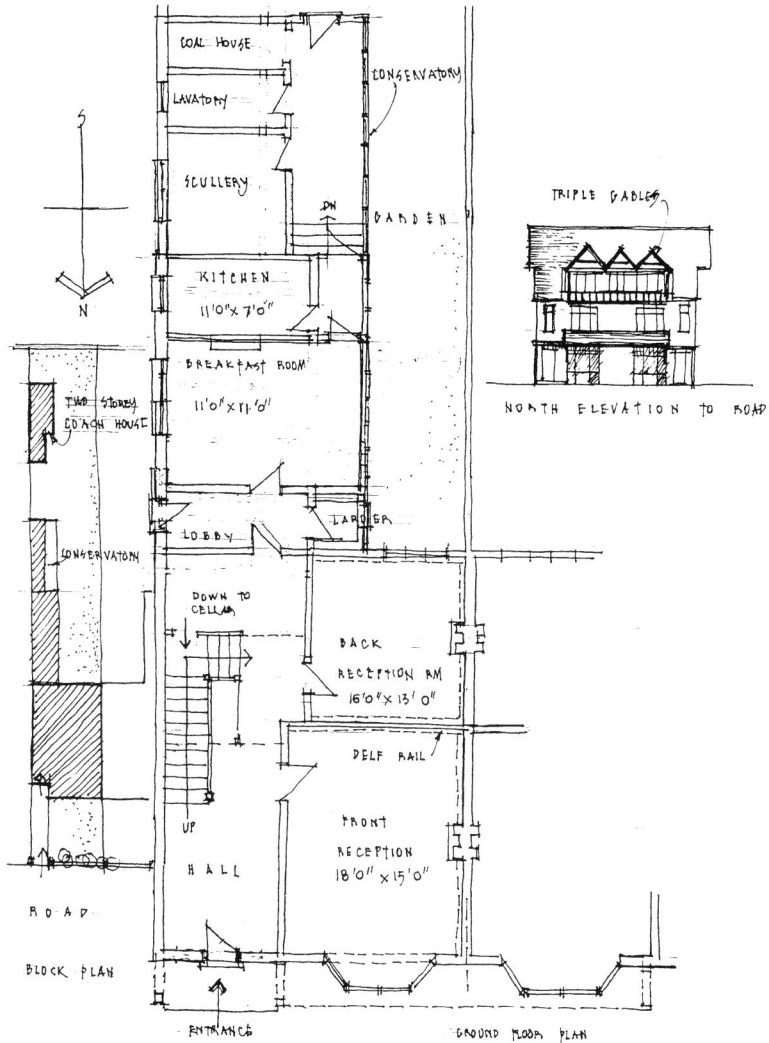

SEMI-DETACHED VILLA WITH COACH HOUSE (1885)
KNIGHTON DRIVE — STONEYGATE : WEST
ARCHITECT : ISAAC BARRADALE

GRANT PITCHES '96

Details of plaster work and lead panels, Inglewood (Helen Boynton)

The second example, the "Bishop's House", is less formal in its architectural geometry. Its key feature is a dramatic corner turret with a conical tiled roof and wide circular eaves. Again, tile hanging is employed to link the heavy mullioned curved windows of the ground and first floors. The house also includes features of exquisite quality and design: two fireplaces, one in carved mahogany with Ionic fluted pilasters and heavily moulded cornice and frieze, the other in grey and white marble, with semi-circular pilasters, capped in black marble; and finally the carved floral door panel in wood.

There is an interesting house on **Stoneygate Avenue**, built in 1901 and designed by Goddard, Goddard and Catlow. It has strong echoes of "Inglewood", built by Ernest Gimson on Ratcliffe Road. Materials include a graded Swithland slate roof, and ferruginous oolitic limestone for the stone trimmings to the doors and windows. The original owner of a large section of this area was Sir Robert Tempest.

Knighton Drive was cut in 1880, and is bordered by a very mixed range of houses dating from the mid-Victorian period to the late 20th century. According to a G. F. Brown and Son sales brochure in 1929, "Knighton Drive, Leicester, occupies an exceedingly convenient situation in this favoured residential locality, within a few minutes walk of the Car Service". It features two groups of interesting semi-detached villas, one by Isaac Barradale (1885), the other by A. E. and T. Sawday.

The former is three-storied, with three linked and bracketed half-timbered gables, in the English Revival style, and exudes the confident status of the original owners, two brothers. The key feature of the interior is the spacious handling of the entrance hall, and the open-well staircase and associated landings. The staircase incorporates a series of beautifully carved newel posts which create a vertical visual rhythm.

The latter, "Oatlands", was owned by A. Tyler J.P., a director of the Wolsey hosiery company. It was brilliantly planned on a tight narrow site, which opened dramatically into a "charming leisure garden comprising a full size tennis court... a rose garden having a lead fountain surrounded by eight frogs and lizards, and a Rose Pergola leading to a garden pavilion..." (Sales brochure 1929). The garden has since been built on, but the villas remain in excellent condition.

On **Elms Road** is one of the most spectacular houses in the tradition of the Arts and Crafts movement is "Knighton Lodge" (1891 - DMU), designed by Joseph Goddard. Set in a garden of about four acres, "the house is approached by a Carriage Sweep with Two Entrance Gates". It was owned by William Evans, boot manufacturer, whose works were in Brunswick Street. The site, excluding the immediate garden, was subsequently sold off as half acre plots for development in the 1920s.

The three-storey house is dominated by the roof, with its large projecting half-timbered gables to the principal elevations and chimney stacks with diaper brickwork. A significant horizontal element to these facades is the deeply projected and rich cornice which acts as a base to the half-timbered top floor. No expense has been spared in the choice of mahogany for the primary features of the interior, such as the elaborate open-well staircase and fireplaces with Fumed Mahogany Mantels. The staircase is lit by an eight-panel stained glass window. Adjoining the house was a charming Loggia or Tea House, and a span roof Orchid House". The "miniature Estate" is completed by a "Capital Paddock".

On the junction of Elms Road and **Ratcliffe Road** is "Inglewood" (1892), designed by Ernest Gimson. It is one of the few listed buildings in Stoneygate, and is nationally famous. The theme of the design is simplicity. The brickwork, however, is enriched by diaper patterning, and the bay window, a later feature, incorporates richly tooled lead panels which include Dutch scenes and birds. The interior includes elaborate plasterwork friezes to the dining room with matching fruit themes to the soffit of the transverse beams.

The architectural practice of Stockdale Harrison and Son designed two particularly historically interesting houses on Elms Road. Stockdale Harrison's contribution was in a "manorial" style (1894), but Shirley Harrison, influenced on this occasion by C. F. A. Voysey, designed

Tile details (left) Knighton Hayes; and carved pargetting and plaster work, The Knowle (Helen Boynton)

"Four Gables" (1910) for his own occupation. This house pursues two themes: horizontalism and the power of the gable.

Occupying a "retired" position on the corner of **Shirley Road** and **Ridgeway Road,** "Braybrook" (1908) was the first house in the development of Shirley Road, as indicated in a Warner Sheppard and Wade sales brochure in September 1927. The original photograph of the garden facade shows a modestly designed brick house with an asymmetrical projecting half-timbered gabled wing, counter-balanced in design by the tall Arts and Crafts chimneys.

However, it is the garden which is particularly interesting as an example of late Edwardian middle class social values, and the importance of providing for leisure within the home setting. The "Pleasure Grounds" include a full-sized tennis lawn, flanked by "Terraced Walks, Rose and Flower Beds, Rock Work etc." Emphasis is placed on the profusion of matured shrubs and trees "ensuring complete privacy".

Details of porches, Knighton Spinneys (left) and Ratcliffe Lodge (Helen Boynton)

De Montfort University (DMU), formerly Leicester Polytechnic, has been one of the principal guardians of some of the finest houses of the late Victorian period on Ratcliffe Road. Many of the interior features have been carefully preserved. "Knighton Hayes" (1881) was built to the design of the Leicester architect Edward Burgess and is a good example of his work. The owner was Mrs Rachael Ellis.

This is another example of the "miniature estate", with a total site area of about 18 acres. The eight acre grounds to the house, "planned with taste and judgement, include the Tennis Lawn" and a "charming shaded Walk through the Shrubberies". A photograph of the carriage entrance gives a clear flavour of the style, in the tradition of English Revival, manorial in detail typified by the heavy mullioned-windows, a quartet of gables, and large scale chimney stacks. It was built of Woodville red bricks, with dressings, and a Swithland slate roof.

Detail of gold-painted fireplace panel, Ava Nursing Home (Helen Boynton)

Bell board, Knighton Spinneys (Helen Boynton)

The schedule and grouping of rooms gives an insight into the hierarchy of the middle class family of this period. They underline the clear separation between the family and the servants: three "Entertaining Rooms"; four bedrooms and two dressing rooms "approached by a wide oak stair", separated from the domestic offices with their "Back Hall and Back Staircase".

A prominent feature of Town End Close (DMU) is the large scale billiard room. Its principal feature is the internal stained glass window to this room, with its delicate brass fittings.

The architect of "Wavertree" (1897 - DMU) was probably Joseph Goddard; it has all the hallmarks of his Arts and Crafts phase. The main entrance is a powerful study in the half-timbering geometry of this style. It has a charming entrance porch with generous hand-carved barge boards to its eaves. Internally, one of the most entrancing features is the staircase with its bowed landing and "crown" capped newel posts. "The Knowle" (DMU) was built in red brick, with a graded Swithland slate roof. Its "Baroque" curved brick parapets to the gables set the tone of rich detailing. One of the key architectural features is the horizontal banding of the bedroom windows with infill panels of carved pargetting.

The interior is particularly rich in architectural detail. In the entrance hall the principal doorway features a tympanum above with elaborately carved plasterwork including an angel's head to the "keystone". The Ionic capitals to the columns in the hall are beautifully carved, including a quirky open swag linking the scrolls. Stained glass windows abound, and often often incorporate phrases: in one fanlight, for example, "For Hospitality and Friendship and Health to all", and in another window "Pleasures are like Poppies Spread".

"Ratcliffe Lodge" (1897 - DMU) was designed by Joseph Goddard. He was probably influenced by Ernest Gimson's "Inglewood" built five years earlier. It shares some of its key features, but the entrance porch has a different flavour and shows Goddard's flair in timber detailing.

"Knighton Spinneys" (1886 - now converted into private flats) was designed by Joseph Goddard for his own occupation. This is probably one of the most spectacular houses on Ratcliffe Road, and the accommodation provided was luxurious even by Goddard's standards. It included a double drawing room, 27 ft x 15 ft and 16 ft x 14 ft, with doors to a garden verandah; nine bedrooms, a "handsome" billiard room and a "Fine Ball or Recreation Room" of 46 ft x 20 ft. The estate, of approximately three acres, was protected by "a pretty Entrance Lodge for Chauffeur", and "the whole property is rendered private by Timber Plantations on three sides".

The overall architectural flavour of the design is dominated by half-timbered walls and gables of the English Domestic Revival style. Its entrance porch, reminiscent of the prow of a ship, projected the confident social status of the owner. The cost of the elaborate interior details, the moulded ceilings to the drawing rooms, and intricate carving to the Indian fireplace in the billiard room alcove, all affirmed his wealth. One of the most powerful indicators of the scale of the house is provided by the bell board. Here is a microcosm of Victorian middle class social success.

A significant number of large villas in Oadby and Stoneygate are still privately owned, but the pattern of ownership has been changing. In addition to those acquired by the universities in the 1970s and 1980s, others have more recently been converted for use as residential homes or day centres for the elderly.

Two such houses of architectural interest are located on Ratcliffe Road. "Manorcroft" (now LOROS Day Centre) was designed for Ernest Lillie, an elastic webbing manufacturer. This cream-rendered house is interesting architecturally, having echoes of C.F.A. Voysey. It is Neo-Georgian in style, with its characteristic vertical sliding sash windows featuring strongly on all facades.

"Ava", now the Ava Nursing Home, still retains an exquisite fireplace made of Italian marble with a central wood panel painted in gold. Both organisations have taken great care to retain the external quality of the buildings, but for obvious functional reasons the interiors have been altered.

THE WEST END AND WESTERN PARK

The setting

The West End and the Western Park area adjoin each other two to two and a half miles (3-4KM) west of the centre of Leicester. The height of the area varies from 61m O.D. at Westcotes Drive to 76m O.D. at Letchworth Road. On Letchworth Road, houses were laid out on a south-facing outcrop ridge of sandstone of Triassic age. They overlook Western Park, where pinkish-brown sandstone is exposed. This can be seen in the valley side opposite. The brook in the valley below Letchworth Road flows through red Mercia Mudstones. To the north east, on Glenfield Road, the sandstone band is overlain with boulder clay.

The Letchworth Road site was particularly suitable for housing development, being on light sandy well-drained soils with a sunny aspect. The land developed in this area was originally part of the Mellor Estate, known as Goose Hill and Slater's Field. The south west side, with its sunny aspect and fine views over the park, was developed first and contains the most interesting of the high quality houses built on the road. It is perhaps surprising that this has not yet been designated a conservation area.

Letchworth Road owes its name to the garden city development at Letchworth, Herts., which clearly influenced its developers. Its upper middle class clientele was attracted to

'LYNDHURST' LETCHWORTH ROAD LEICESTER (PLANS: 1915)
ARCHITECT : ERNEST HENRY SMITH

71

the area because it bordered Western Park, then at the western extent of the city. Westcotes Drive takes its name from the Westcotes estate, former home of the Ruding family, sold for development in the 1880s.

All the roads leading westwards off Narborough Road have an uphill gradient, caused by an outlier of Triassic sandstone, which is capped by glacial gravels and boulder clay. This elongated hill is about one mile long and has produced some excellent well-drained building

House on Ashleigh Road (Leslie Orton)

sites, particularly at the upper end of Westcotes Drive which is now a conservation area. A crucial factor in the design of houses on the Letchworth Road ridge is the dramatic slope of the building sites generated. This gives the architect both a major constraint and a great opportunity for creative design. For instance, a basement might be both a leisure and a service resource, and the reception rooms and main bedrooms could be planned to have superb middle-distance views over the valley across Western Park.

Significant houses

There are two houses of exceptional quality and historic interest on **Letchworth Road**: "Lyndhurst" (plans dated 1915), designed by a young architect called Ernest Henry Smith; and "Summer Hill" (1909) by the local architect W. R. Bedingfield. "Lyndhurst" was first owned by William Merryfield Matthews, a boot manufacturer, whose brief to the architect required lavish accommodation, even incorporating a ballroom in the basement. One of the most interesting features of the house is the use of the cantilever as an element in its construction: the elevation to the garden incorporates a powerful cantilevered gable.

"Summer Hill" also optimises on the drama of the site, and is an example of a beautifully resolved curved geometry. This, and some other aspects of this architect's domestic designs in Leicester, show the influence of C. F. A. Voysey, whose house "Broadleys" (1889), on the edge of Lake Windermere, displays bow-windowed bedrooms planned to take advantage of the views, seemingly echoed here in the ingeniously arranged rooms at "Summer Hill". The sale brochure by the estate agent for this house, suggests the importance attached to the concept of "fresh air and health" by the middle class culture of the time.

Another more modest example of Bedingfield's work is a pair of semi-detached houses located close to the two houses described above. It illustrates a very neat solution to the problem of "duality", which besets the design of semi-detached dwellings. By creating a dominant central gable as a symmetrical focus to the road facade, he has given a pleasing unity to the scheme. Emphasis is given here to the gable by its rough-cast finish, in contrast to the brickwork of the ground floor and the bedroom wings.

There were two significantly different types of development in the **Westcotes Drive** area: long terrace houses, built between 1903-1907, and large scale villas such as "Sykefield", "Westcotes Lodge", "Bradgate House" and "Westcotes Grange". The architect of "Sykefield" (1882), an unusually powerful study in the Arts and Crafts idiom, was Ewan Christian of London who also designed St. Mark's church in Leicester. It features a massive complex graded-slate roof, heavy-mullioned windows, and the tall elaborate chimneys of this style. The porch to the main entrance is well detailed and includes mullions of oolitic shelly limestone. The gardens to this large villa are enclosed with a high brick boundary wall, an indication of the obsession with privacy of the wealthy middle class of this period.

"Westcotes Grange" was built in 1869 to the design of the famous architect S. S. Teulon (1812-1873). He was based in London and was responsible for an extensive

Detail of angel's head, Ashleigh Road, and carved detail of porch, Westleigh Road (Helen Boynton)

range of churches and houses in Britain, including Holy Trinity Church in Regent Road, Leicester. The purple brickwork used in Westcotes Grange is alien to the local region which is characterised by red bricks, but is well detailed. Another significant villa, now called "Bradgate House", was built in 1907 for John Russell Frears, the biscuit manufacturer. "Westcotes Lodge" (now West Leicester Conservative Club) is an Edwardian house designed for the footwear manufacturer J. G. Chattaway. The architect is unknown. The entrance hall features a deep cornice of elaborate plaster work and a beautiful stained glass landing window.

The architectural theme of lower **Ashleigh Road**, a conservation area is the large three-storey terrace interspersed with similar scale semi-detached villas. Its special quality is the consistency of the rich detailing of the bay windows, and giant deep projecting gables with their richly-moulded barge boards. One of the earliest houses on Ashleigh Road was "West Leigh", built in 1867 for Archibald Turner, elastic web manufacturer.

There is a similar theme to Westleigh Road, which takes its name from Turner's house. Although more diverse in the range of styles, the overriding impression is one of high quality building by contractors employing craftsmen who took pride in their work. A feature of a number of the houses is the use of stained glass in porches and some windows.

WIGSTON FIELDS, WIGSTON MAGNA AND SOUTH WIGSTON.

The setting

South Wigston is approximately four and a half miles (7KM) south of Leicester at a height of 76m O.D. It is located on the Lower Lias shales and clays which occur in the valley sides of a small tributary flowing southwards to join the River Sence. These clays have been excavated for brick-clay, and the bricks used for building schemes in South Wigston by the Leicester builder Orson Wright.

Wigston Magna is located on glacial gravels, approximately four miles (6KM) south of Leicester at a height of about 100m O.D.. It was easily accessible by rail from the town in the later 19th century, and proved attractive to developers and builders. Wigston Fields is the area to the north west of Wigston Magna.

Significant houses

The most interesting house of this period, in South Wigston, "The Vicarage", was designed by Stockdale Harrison. It is not as flamboyant as his usual approach, but the main facade demonstrates his liking for asymmetrical design. The central feature - with its

Bushloe House, Wigston, pictured in a sale brochure

semicircular gable and main entrance door to the right and the three-light windows to the left - is counterbalanced by the chimney stack on the right. The blue-brick string-courses to the facades help unify all these elements.

There are three houses of particular interest in this area. "The Firs" in Wigston Field has undergone many changes in layout and style, but in its entrance hall it still includes a remarkable staircase in mahogany, the special feature of which is a double-newel post of exquisite quality. The house was owned in the recent past by the rose grower Harry Wheatcroft.

The second house is a local landmark. "Bushloe House" on **Station Road**, currently the offices of Oadby and Wigston Borough Council, was owned by H. A. Owston. The two property was "within a few minutes walk of the Railway Station on the Midland Main Line, about one mile from South Wigston Station on the Rugby Branch of the Midland Railway, and four miles from Leicester". It was built in whitish-beige brick and stone, and designed in a heavy eclectic style with powerful mullioned windows. Its main feature is its dominant slated roof which incorporates large dormer windows.

The accommodation reflected the middle class lifestyle of the period and included a library (15 x 14 ft) "fitted with Ebonized Bookcases in recesses", and a Billiard Room (26 x 20 ft). The domestic offices included a servants' hall and "three Capital Cellars, well lighted, and two Wine Cellars in the basement". There were eight bedrooms, and three servants' bedrooms accessed by a back-stair.

WOODHOUSE EAVES

The setting

Woodhouse Eaves is approximately six miles (10K) north west of the centre of Leicester, at a height of 107-152m O.D.. The village is located on the eastern limb of the Charnian anticline, and many of its houses are constructed using local slates, sandstones and conglomerates in attractive purplish black and orange-stained colours. Many are also roofed with Swithland slates, excavated nearby.

Significant houses

Pevsner, in his "Buildings of England: Leicestershire & Rutland" (1960), dismisses the domestic architecture of Woodhouse Eaves in a sentence: "In Maplewell Road a number of cottages built of rough stones from the Swithland Slate pits". There are in fact a number of significant late Victorian and Edwardian houses in Woodhouse Eaves by well known local architects of the period - and one by a national architect. The scale of these houses, combined with the tranquil and elevated setting, later made them ideal for use as nursing and

Maplewell Hall (Grant Pitches)

convalescent homes. However, there are some historically interesting ones still in private ownership.

"Maplewell Hall", on **Maplewell Road**, is now a school for children with moderate learning difficulties. The estate formerly belonged to Miss W. L. Fox, of the Fox's Glacier Mints family. According to a 1946 sales brochure, it consisted of 171 acres of land, plus the house itself and a number of small cottages and farms. The house, which was restored c.1870, is built in local Charnian stone with Jurassic oolitic limestone mullions and quoins and a Swithland slate roof. The exterior is dominated by pairs of large gables on the main entrance and garden frontages.

Internally, the large entrance hall has a massive oak mantlepiece and panelled ceiling. In the sale brochure it is recorded that there were five elegant rooms leading from the main lounge hall with marble fireplaces. An interesting item was a Three Manual Pipe Organ in Oak case, by Large and Foster, Sheffield with organ chamber in the rear. Included in the estate were stables and farm buildings, tennis and croquet lawns, three carnation houses, a vinery, and pleasure grounds of "rare Sylvan beauty". The fine Old-English walled kitchen garden had a lean-to peach house and 'a range of three-span cucumber and melon houses".

"Charnwood House", on **Brand Hill**, was originally the Cooper Memorial Homes for Sick Children. A plaque over the door bears the inscription "Given by the Rev. W. H. Cooper, of Burleigh Hall, Loughborough in memory of his wife Mary Cooper 1900". Architecturally, it has a Neo-Georgian flavour, with a five-bay balconied first floor feature to the main entrance. It is now a residential home

for the elderly. A second holiday home, "Maplehurst", was built on **Post Office Drive** in 1899. It was designed by Stockdale Harrison for the Leicester stockbroker Sir Arthur Wheeler. The half-timbered projection was added by Shirley Harrison in the 1930's.

"Patchwood" on **Church Hill** was designed by J. Goddard in 1908 for O. L. Arnall. Architecturally, this is a delightful design incorporating bay windows to the principal rooms, and featuring triple linked gables to the entrance elevation. Its rendered walls provide an ideal contrast to the Swithland slate roof. "Swithland Court" (c.1906) was originally built as a convalescent home, in red brick with ironstone mullions and quoins. It has a Charnian slate wall in front of the main door, with steps and a fountain. It is now private flats, but the lodge at the foot of the hill drive is still standing.

"The Brand" was built in 1875, and designed by the nationally famous London architect, Alfred Waterhouse (1830-1905) for Alfred Ellis of John Ellis and Co., coal merchants. It was sold in 1887, along with the "Wheatsheaf Cottages", nearby, for £11,000. The sale brochure of that date notes it was "situated on the borders of Charnwood Forest within three miles of the Quorn Hunt". Society in the neighbourhood "is most select, the seats of noblemen and landed gentry surrounding the property".

Alfred Waterhouse was one of the leading Victorian architects, and designed a wide range of prestigious buildings - civic, commercial and ecclesiastical. This house is relatively modest in style, but has the characteristic Waterhouse quality of detailing. It is built of local Charnian stone with fine red sandstone mullions

**Garden front, The Brand
(Helen Boynton)**

and quoins. It has a Swithland slate roof, with large scale gables to the garden facade. The water supply was derived from rock pools and pumped by a large steam engine to a higher reservoir, to descend to the house under high pressure. The kitchen garden included two vineries, along with melon, cucumber and mushroom houses.

House on London Road (London Road Hospital), with Lyndwood (now demolished) in background, c.1908 (Helen Boynton)

LEICESTER'S SUBURBAN GARDENS:

FROM VILLA TO MINIATURE ESTATE

"Space (was) designed to secure privacy from onlookers"[1]

At the end of the 19th century, the design of the large garden in Britain was a contentious issue. The two key opponents in the debate were William Robinson (1838-1935), a self-made prestigious gardener and author, and the architect Reginald Blomfield (1856-1942).

The issue centred on whether the house and garden should be designed as an integral unit, or whether the house should be an independent element in the garden. The former approach generated the "formal garden" advocated by Blomfield., who favoured "the refinement and reserve of the 17th century garden"; and the latter, promoted by Robinson, the "natural garden".

The layout of later Edwardian gardens was generally a blend of these two approaches. In his book "The Edwardian Garden" (1989), David Ottewill points out that "what gave the Edwardian garden its unique quality was a combination of formal layout with exuberant" informal planting". One of the underlying themes of Edwardian houses and gardens was the obsession of the owners with space and privacy. This was manifest in the scale of the larger gardens, the nature of enclosure and their "components"; leisure facilities such as croquet and tennis lawns, for example.

The suburbs of Leicester encompass a wide spectrum of gardens, which can be broadly classified into four main groups: the villa garden; those of the small detached house; the medium size garden of between two and four acres acres (0.8-1.6ha); and the "miniature estates" of between four and eight acres (1.6-3.2ha).

The gardens of the three-storey, semi-detached and terraced villas, were less than a quarter of an acre (0.1ha) in area. There are numerous examples to be found in Leicester and its suburbs: in Stoneygate Road, Knighton Drive, Loughborough Road, Aylestone Road, Clarendon Park Road, and Ashleigh and Westleigh Roads. These villas were generally occupied by families of "middling" status.

The gardens comprised two distinct zones. The front gardens were usually formal with small neat flower beds. They were often enclosed by elaborate low brick walls with stone-capped brick piers and cast iron ornate infill panels. The aspect of the gardens was arbitrary, determined by the street layout. The back gardens varied in treatment and the nature of outbuildings. The houses often had conservatories attached, and at the

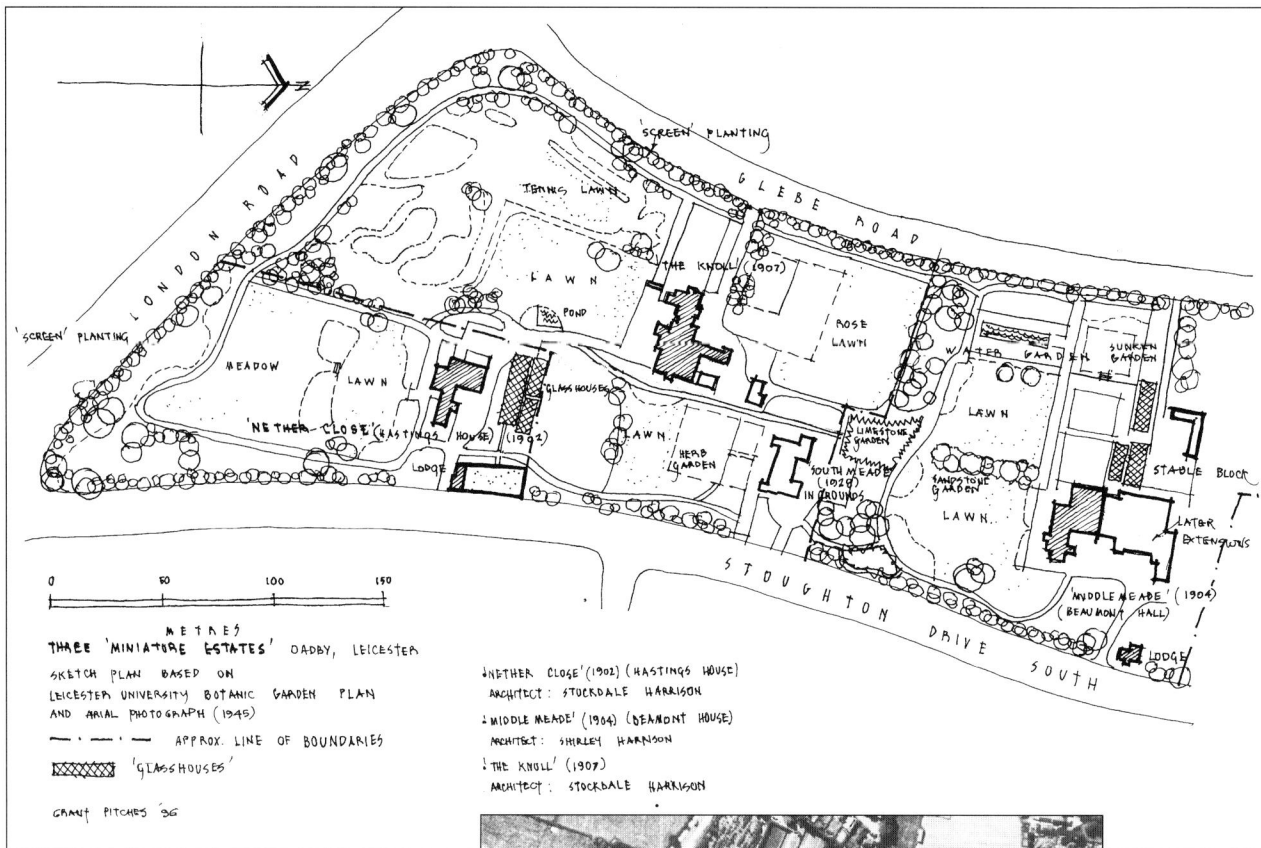

N

SCREEN PLANTING

GLEBE ROAD

LONDON ROAD

TENNIS LAWN

THE KNOLL (1907)

LAWN

ROSE LAWN

SCREEN PLANTING

POND

WINTER GARDEN

SUNKEN GARDEN

MEADOW

LAWN

GLASS HOUSES

NETHER CLOSE (HASTINGS HOUSE) (1902)

LAWN

HERB GARDEN

LIMESTONE GARDEN

LAWN

LODGE

SANDSTONE GARDEN

LAWN

STABLE BLOCK

SOUTH MEADE (1902) IN GROUNDS

LATER EXTENSIONS

STOUGHTON DRIVE SOUTH

MIDDLE MEADE (1904) (BEAUMONT HALL)

LODGE

0   50   100   150

M E T R E S

THREE 'MINIATURE ESTATES' OADBY, LEICESTER

SKETCH PLAN BASED ON
LEICESTER UNIVERSITY BOTANIC GARDEN PLAN
AND ARIAL PHOTOGRAPH (1945)

— · —   APPROX LINE OF BOUNDARIES

⬚⬚⬚⬚   'GLASSHOUSES'

GRANT PITCHES 3G

'NETHER CLOSE' (1902) (HASTINGS HOUSE)
ARCHITECT: STOCKDALE HARRISON

'MIDDLE MEADE' (1904) (BEAMONT HOUSE)
ARCHITECT: SHIRLEY HARRISON

'THE KNOLL' (1907)
ARCHITECT: STOCKDALE HARRISON

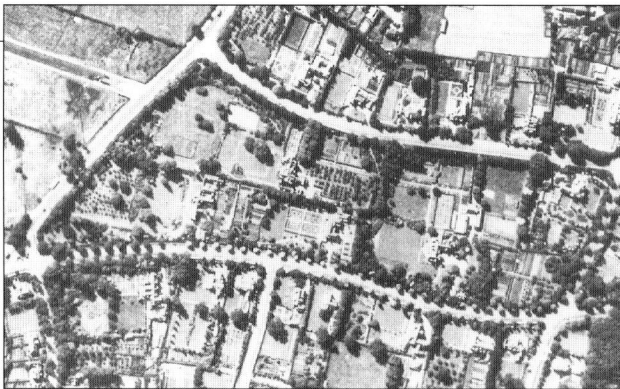

**Aerial view (1945) and plan of
what are now the University of
Leicester Botanical Gardens
formerly the three "miniature
estates" of Nether Close,
Middlemeade and The Knoll
(Grant Pitches)**

end of some of the gardens were combined coach houses and stable blocks. A interesting example of this layout is to be found at a large pair of semi-detached villas in Knighton Drive designed by Isaac Barradale (1885). The coach house included space for the stable boy at first floor level.

The garden of the small detached house, also less than a quarter of an acre (0.1ha) in area, is typified by the development of Meadowcourt Road, Oadby, designed by the Leicester architects A. E. and T. Sawday. The area was formerly part of the Powys-Keck estate, and strict covenants were imposed, including the minimum cost of the houses to be built. The properties were geared to a "solid" middle class group: doctors, architects and small scale industrialists. The aspect of the gardens was also limited by the nature of the road layout. The detailed planting treatment of the gardens was highly variable.

A number of developments of small detached houses capitalised on the views and health benefits of elevated sloping sites. Perhaps one of the most dramatic examples from the late Edwardian period is at Birstall. The section of the Soar valley at this point is asymmetrical, and the river flows right against the hillside, where a steep slope rises up westwards from the river. This was fully utilised by the builders for small and medium houses with terraced gardens.

A classic example of the medium size (2-4 acres/0.8-1.6ha) garden layout is at Kirby Fields, developed by Matthew Brady, boot and shoe manufacturer, at the end of the 19th century. The houses, designed by a number of Leicester architects, were carefully planned to take

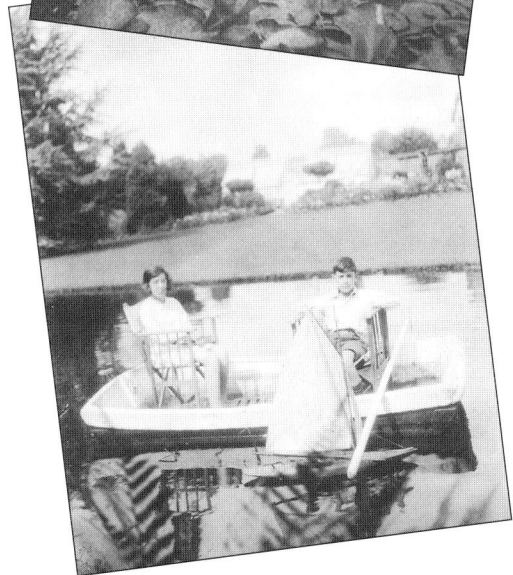

George and Peggy Hurst, and friend, with their niece and nephew, Margaret and Jim Browett (top) who also appear in the second photograph (Jim Browett)

advantage of the preferred south aspect for living spaces. There is no clear pattern of garden design, although some included large pines and monkey puzzle trees. They were essentially "lawn gardens" with minimum formal elements.

The "miniature estate", with a garden of 4-8 acres (1.6-3.2ha), is found in the suburbs of Oadby and Stoneygate, which housed Leicester's wealthiest industrialists and professionals. One of the finest examples is the group of houses and gardens which now constitute the Leicester University Botanic Garden. A scaled down version of the estates of the landed gentry, they incorporated all the components of the late Victorian and Edwardian garden, and reflected the social milieu of the upper middle class of this period. They provide an interesting profile of their values and lifestyle, and warrant a more detailed examination.

One of the key features of these larger gardens was the "leisure garden". This provided the wealthy owners with relaxation from the pressures of business, and a framework for the social life of their families. "The click of croquet balls on the lawn, the murmur of flirtations by the lake... And ah yes, the swish of taffeta skirts on the path between the long herbaceous borders. The large Edwardian house was a background for leisure".[2] The ultimate relaxation for the family was punting or boating, and the lake was a feature of several large gardens in Oadby - including "The Hermitage", "Tetuan" in Manor Road, and "The Knoll" in Glebe Road. The mood and personality of these gardens was strengthened by the informal planting of the herbaceous borders, the highly perfumed rose garden, the herb garden, and frequently a substantial rockery.

These gardens were labour-intensive, and required a number of gardeners - ranging from highly skilled craftsmen to labourers - to cope with the wide range of tasks involved. The social conditions and wages of these workers are described in detail in David Stuart's book "The Garden Triumphant" (1988), but the role of the head gardener was crucial in determining the ambience of the garden: its colour, textures, and above all, its style.

Head gardeners were powerful and could be over-zealous. In "Victorian Gardens" (1986), Brent Elliot quotes Charles Wade, whose garden was designed by Baillie Scott, but was controlled in its planting by the head gardener to such an extent that "it ceased to be our garden anymore". The number of gardeners employed by Leicester's wealthy property owners has been recorded in some instances. At "Middlemeade" in Oadby, there were ten gardeners, both "outdoor" and "indoor". For a smaller garden in Knighton Rise, Oadby, there were three. Their access to the main garden area was often screened by hedges, and literally hidden from the owner's view.

Three "miniature estate" gardens and two smaller gardens may illustrate the unique qualities of the Edwardian garden. "The Hermitage" (1901) in Oadby, owned by the hosiery manufacturer T. G. Hirst and designed by architects Goddard and Catlow, covered an area of just over six acres. This garden encapsulates all the elements of the Edwardian dream of leisure, scale and privacy. According to a sale brochure in the 1930s, it "stands detached on a gravel subsoil, about 316 feet

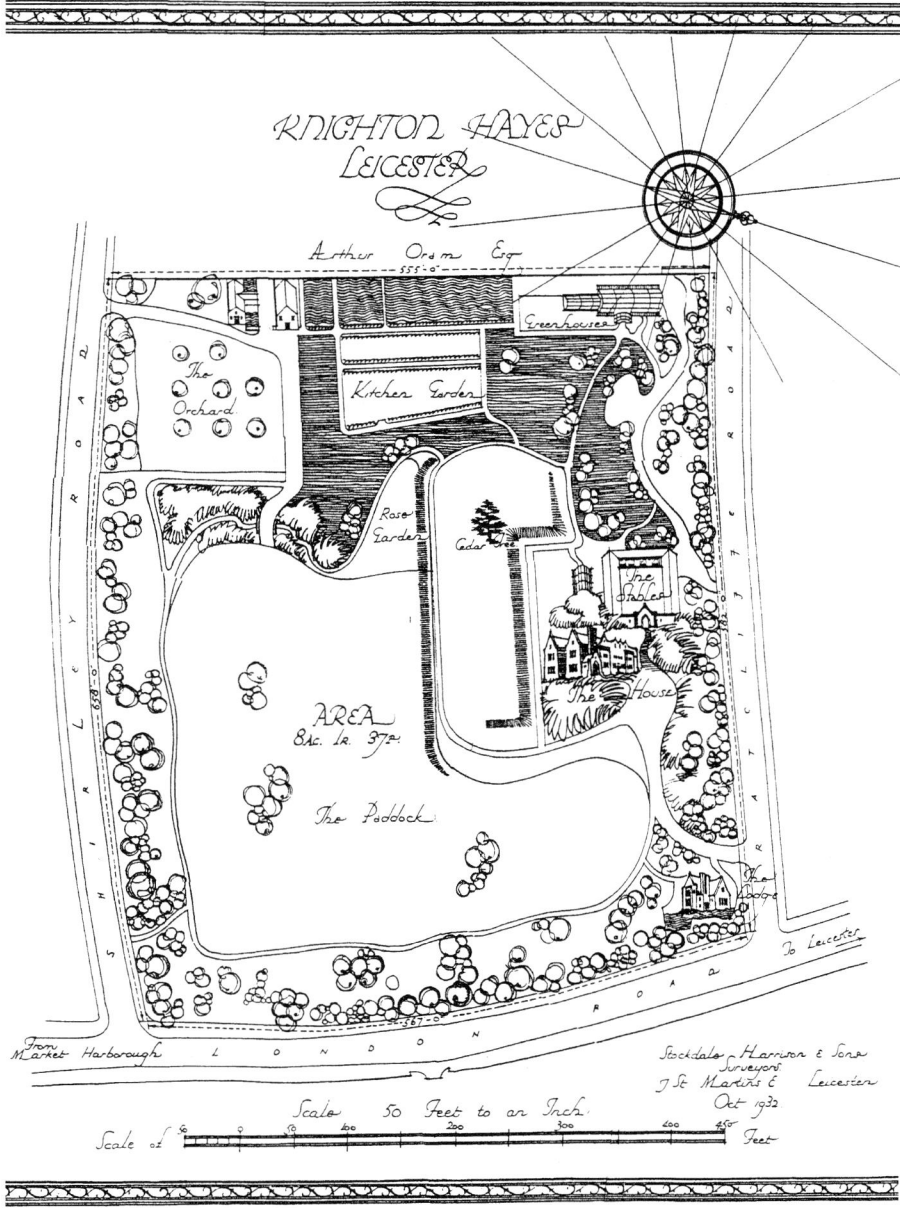

KNIGHTON HAYES
Leicester

Arthur Oram Esq

The Orchard

Kitchen Garden

Greenhouses

Rose Garden

Cedar

The Stables

The House

AREA
8 Ac. 1 R. 37 P.

The Paddock

The Lodge

To Leicester

From Market Harborough

LONDON ROAD

SHIRLEY ROAD

RATCLIFFE ROAD

Stockdale, Harrison & Sons
Surveyors
7 St Martins E Leicester
Oct 1932

Scale 50 Feet to an Inch.
Scale of

Particulars of the Highly Desirable Small Residential Estate

"The Hermitage"
OADBY

"THE HERMITAGE," FROM THE GROUNDS.

FOR SALE BY AUCTION
ON TUESDAY, 22nd SEPTEMBER, 1931
AT THREE O'CLOCK.
AS A WHOLE OR IN LOTS.

Freehold.

Auctioneers :
Messrs. WARNER, SHEPPARD & WADE
and P. L. KIRBY
16 & 18 Halford Street, Leicester.

Solicitors :
Messrs. FREER & Co.
10 New Street,
Leicester.

above sea level, in a retired part of the village, near the Church, with shrubbed forecourt on the front and is protected from the Wigston Road by a high brick wall ensuring absolute privacy".

The general aspect was ideal. "There is a gentle declivity to the South, and the slope down to the margin of the Ornamental Lake… gives a beautiful vista from the principal apartments of the house…" The overall layout of the garden took advantage of the slope, with the wide York stone terrace of the house linked to a large "Pleasure Lawn" set with forest trees, leading down to a croquet lawn which terminated on the edge of a fish-filled lake. The family used the lake for boating picnics over the summer months.

The "Birstall Holt" estate (1872) covered over 15 acres and comprised an eight bedroom house, a cottage with nine "bed and dressing rooms" and its own one and a quarter acre garden, and a stable bloc set in fourteen and a half acres of "rich old turf land". Unlike "The Hermitage", it was a "natural" garden, of a design which would have found favour with Robinson: "charming pleasure grounds" of a "natural Park-like appearance" studded with a large number of forest trees.

"Knighton Hayes" (1881) in Stoneygate was designed by the local architect Edward Burgess for the Ellis family. This is another interesting example of a "natural" garden, in which there is little attempt even to create formal terraces adjacent to the house. There is merely a grass bank forming the edge to the lawn, linked to an informal rose garden. The dominant feature of the eight acre garden is a three acre paddock, edged with screening trees to the adjacent roads. The kitchen garden, greenhouses, and the orchard constitute about two acres on the west of the site.

In contrast to these large scale houses and gardens, a small late Edwardian garden in a "middle class" development in Oadby, designed by T. E. Sawday and Son, typifies the blend of formal and informal layout of a garden of this scale and date. "Meadow Croft" on Meadowcourt Road, Oadby (c.1925), was designed by the Leicester architect Cyril Ogden. The building plots on this road (laid down in 1910) varied significantly in size, from a quarter of an acre for the semi-detached houses at the top of the road to up to half an acre for the larger ones at the London Road end. "Meadow Croft" combines a screened formal garden closely linked to the house, and the separate sunken leisure garden dominated by the tennis court. Privacy is achieved by the enclosing hedges and laurel bushes, and the whole arrangement is quite typical of its time.

The three acre garden at "Highgrove" (1905) in Oadby, probably designed by Stockdale Harrison, is another excellent example of Edwardian garden design, combining formality and informality. The original owner was T. S. Grieve, a manufacturer of needles and knitting machines for the hosiery industry, and the house was later occupied by Sir Holland and Lady Goddard.

Their son, Michael Goddard, recalls that "there was quite a contrast between the formal geometrical layout of the garden between the house and up and including the croquet lawn. Beyond that the lines were curved and informal, consisting in the main of gently sloping terrain with an extensive lawn into which had been set irregularly shaped beds/borders of shrubs and small trees". The formal garden creates a serene mood enhanced by the rectangular pool which terminates the

Cascade of waterfalls, Highgrove (Michael Goddard)

axis of the design. A key feature of this area of the garden is a cascade of seven waterfalls with pools increasing progressively in size down the garden. The gardens were maintained by two full-time gardeners.

References

1. Long H., "The Edwardian House" (1993)
2. Scott-James A., "The Cottage Garden" (1981)

POSTSCRIPT: local issues of architectural conservation

During the 1960s and 1970s a significant number of Victorian and Edwardian buildings were demolished nationally and locally in the development of commercial and housing schemes. Kirby Fields typifies Leicester's sad loss of important housing stock. "Walburton" (1903), the home of Sir Edward Wood, was demolished in 1962; "The Holt" (1916), one of Stockdale Harrison's finest houses, in 1969; and "Rosendene" (1890) built by Sir Edward Wood, in the mid 1970s. A more recent casualty is "Thurnby Grange", once the home of Charles Bennion, Managing Director of the British United Shoe Machinery Company for many years, who in 1928 purchased Bradgate Park and gave it to the people of Leicester and Leicestershire.

After 1945 one of the few guardians of the large Edwardian houses in Leicester was Leicester University, whose enlightened policy on student accommodation ensured that they were retained and sensitively converted to new uses. A similar policy was later pursued by De Montfort University, formerly Leicester Polytechnic. Over the last decade, however, there has been a growth in public awareness of the need to preserve the heritage of 19th and early 20th century buildings, and it is interesting to note that in terms of commercial buildings "listed buildings outperformed all other office buildings in a survey of rental growth" (Building Design, 2 February 1996).

However, while listing of listing of historic buildings has been largely carried out, we believe that there is a need to give more priority to identifying gardens of the Victorian, Edwardian and post-Edwardian periods which have retained their structure and features. We discovered some remarkable gardens which still include their post-Edwardian elements. For example, in Meadowcourt Road, Oadby, a formal garden is enclosed in a beautiful geometric yew hedge which is in excellent condition. The structure is also evident in the York stone paths which form the "skeleton" of the layout.

The period from 1900 to the mid 1920s was one of the richest in Britain in terms of garden design, when the work of the architect Edwin Lutyens and Gertrude Jekyll, the artist-gardener who created about two hundred gardens, provided models for provincial garden designers and architects. It is a desert in terms of listed medium scale gardens of one or two acres, and we feel that it is time that this rich heritage of gardens is recognised both by English Heritage and local authorities. However, a branch of the Association of Garden Trusts is shortly to be set up in Leicestershire and Rutland. This organisation already operates in 25 counties, and is devoted to recording, researching and preserving historic gardens.

In the context of large scale Edwardian houses and gardens, another issue which has surfaced is the environmental impact of conversions and extensions. If we are to retain the visual and environmental quality of these sensitive areas, it is important that local authorities encourage developers to liaise with appropriate professionals such as architects and landscape architects, at outline planning stage.

Both Leicester City Council and Leicestershire County Council have defined designated Conservation Areas. The "Action Plan" for the New Walk Conservation Area in Leicester is a model of its kind; but in our survey of the suburbs we have identified one area of exceptional quality - Letchworth Road - which has not been included in the designated conservation area lists. Most of these houses fortunately have not been modernised, and so far have largely retained their original architectural features.

Finally, in examining future conservation policies, we feel that it is essential that houses and gardens, both individually and in group or area contexts, should be perceived as entities and not in isolation. Leicester and its suburbs embrace a rich heritage of late Victorian and Edwardian houses and gardens. Let us, the vigilant general public, through the agencies of local authorities and voluntary organisations such as the Victorian Society, ensure that they remain protected from insensitive development for future generations.

Appendix 1
GLOSSARY OF ARCHITECTURAL TERMS

ARTS AND CRAFTS MOVEMENT: A 19th century movement in Britain evolved as a reaction to the devaluation of craftsmanship. Its central aim was to bring together not only architects and designers, but craftsmen, to develop, at a reasonable cost, well made and desirous objects. In reality, the items produced were highly expensive and only affordable by the upper middle classes.

BALUSTER: a post in a balustrade of a staircase. There is a wide range of design: for example, circular or square in section (in the style of Voysey), or even "barley-sugar".

BRICK BOND: the form of structural brickwork. There are two common bonds: "Stretcher", using the bricks longitudinally as stretchers; and "English, using stretchers and headers in alternate courses.

BUTTRESS: an angled support of brick or stonework to give structural stability

CANTILEVER: A projecting beam or beams, stabilised by continuity of construction.

CORNICE: an external or internal moulding formed at the top of a wall.

CUPOLA: a roof feature in the form of a small turret.

DIAPER: pattern of brickwork based on the diagonal.

EAVES: the projection of the roof.

ECLECTIC: a mixture of styles in one building or facade.

ELEVATION: architect's term for the detailed drawing of each side of a building, related to aspect, eg. north elevation.

FINIAL: an ornament fixed at the top of a gable or roof.

FROG: an indentation in the top of a brick to lighten its weight.

GABLE: the triangular part of the upper section of a wall.

HALF-TIMBERED: usually refers to architecture in which the timber frame is fixed onto a structural wall.

HEADER: the exposed end of a brick used to bond the wall together.

HIPPED ROOF: a roof with four sloping edges instead of the more traditional four.

MULLION: vertical element dividing a window, usually in stone. **TRANSOM** is the horizontal equivalent.

NEWEL POST: a post supporting the ends of the "strings" and handrail of a staircase. These were often highly elaborate in form in the late Victorian period, hand carved in mahogany or oak.

ORDERS of ARCHITECTURE: used in Classical and Neo-Classical styles, they comprise a column with base, shaft, capital and entablature. There are various styles, details of which are complex. These are: Greek Doric, Roman Doric, Tuscan Doric, Ionic, Corinthian and Composite.

PEDIMENT: a low-pitched gable of Greek and Roman origin.

PILASTER: a slightly projecting profiled column integral with the wall face.

QUEEN ANNE REVIVAL: misleading title for a hybrid style of architecture (1870s-early 1900s) adopted by the middle class, combining 17th and 18th century features such as "Flemish" gables and steeply pitched roofs.

QUOINS: coursed stonework or brickwork used on the corners of buildings.

RAINWATER HEAD: box-like fitting, used to collect water from the gutters fixed to the eaves.

RENDERING: a "skin" of waterproof plaster or cement applied to external walls.

STAINED GLASS: a misleading term for coloured glass. The colour is fired into the glass.

STAIR "STRING": an angled board, grooved to receive and support the treads of a stair.

STRING COURSE: horizontal, slightly projecting band of brick or stonework formed on external walls.

VERNACULAR ARCHITECTURE: buildings dated usually before about 1850, using local building materials.

WINDOWS: the basic categories are as follows:
 Casement: side-hung on vertical hinges
 Sliding Sash: vertically hung - slide up and down
 Dormer: a vertical window located on a sloping roof.
 Oriel: an upper storey projecting window.
 Venetian: a triple-light window with raised semi-circular middle unit.

Appendix 2
GLOSSARY OF GEOLOGICAL TERMS

ALLUVIUM: fine-grained muds and silts laid by rivers during flooding over the low flat land on either side. This flat land is known as the **FLOOD PLAIN**.

CLEAVAGE: natural plane of splitting of the Swithland Slates.

CURRENT BEDDING: concave curved bedding seen in sandstones and limestones, which indicates they were laid down by current actions in the shallow sea water.

DIORITES: igneous rocks found in Charnwood Forest, Enderby Quarries and other locations. Solidified below the earth's surface from molten magma, and uncovered by later weathering. Similar in some respects to granite.

FIRECLAYS: (or Seat Earths). Fossil soils below the coal seams in the Leicestershire coalfield, found in the Coalville area.

FLOOD PLAIN: low flat land on either side of a river. This is not generally suitable for building because of flooding.

GEOLOGICAL COLUMN: a longitudinal column of the systems of rocks, from the oldest at the bottom to the youngest at the top. It shows the division of geological time.

GLACIAL DEPOSITS: sands, gravels and boulder clays which were laid down during the Pleistocene period when the ice sheets covered the country as far south as the River Thames.

LIMONITE: brown iron oxide mineral.

LOWER LIAS CLAYS: of the **JURASSIC SYSTEM**. Stiff, dark bluish-grey clays and grey limestones with fossil bivalves and ammonites

MERCIA MUDSTONES (KEUPER MARL): limy muds consisting of reddish-brown clays and interspersed pale-green bands. The red marls were used extensively in brick-making during the Victorian and Edwardian period.

POROSITY: the closeness of grains and amount of air space in a rock.

RHAETIC BEDS: thin dark-grey shales, only rarely exposed in excavations or boreholes in Leicester. They give rise to the hill on London Road up to Victoria Park, and the hill on Uppingham Road from Humberstone Park.

RIVER TERRACES: areas of generally flat land on either side of a river at a higher level than the flood plain. They consist of sands and gravels laid down by the river when it flowed at a higher level. These river terraces are not continuous, but where they occur they have made ideal building sites, as they are generally well-drained and springs can occur at their junction with the overlying strata.

TRIASSIC SANDSTONES: thin bands within the **MERCIA MUDSTONES** or Keuper Marls. They are light-brownish red in colour and form prominent ridges or higher ground in the West End of Leicester, eg. Westcotes Drive, and Letchworth Road overlooking Western Park.

STRATA: beds of rocks which may be horizontal or inclined.

SWITHLAND SLATES: fine grained muddy sediments which accumulated in the sea at the end of the Pre-Cambrian period. These consolidated and hardened to form greenish-grey slates.

Appendix 3
GEOLOGICAL COLUMN

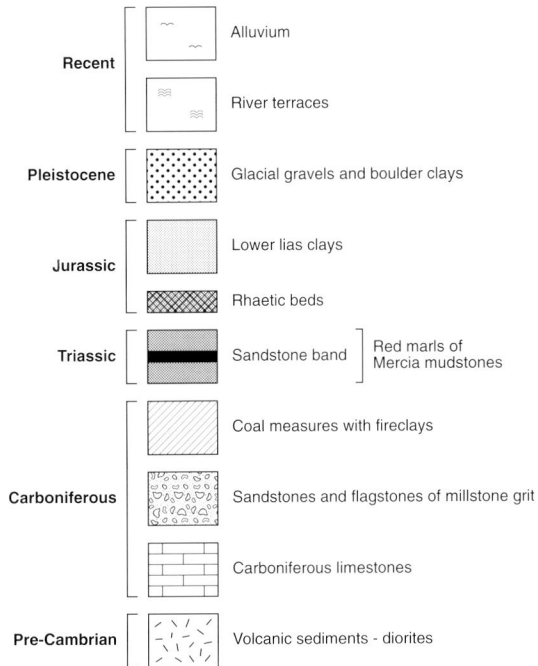

Recent		Alluvium
		River terraces
Pleistocene		Glacial gravels and boulder clays
Jurassic		Lower lias clays
		Rhaetic beds
Triassic		Sandstone band — Red marls of Mercia mudstones
Carboniferous		Coal measures with fireclays
		Sandstones and flagstones of millstone grit
		Carboniferous limestones
Pre-Cambrian		Volcanic sediments - diorites

Appendix 4
CONSERVATION AREAS IN THE CITY OF LEICESTER

Ashleigh Road
Aylestone Village
Belgrave Hall
Braunstone Village
Castle Gardens
Cathedral/Guildhall
Daneshill
Evington Footpath
Evington Village
High Street
Highfields, South
Humberstone, Old
Knighton Village
Loughborough Road
Market Place
Market Street
New Walk
St. George's
Spinney Hill Park
Stoneygate
Town Hall Square
Westcotes Drive

Conservation areas in the county of Leicestershire include Birstall; Oadby: Hill Top and Meadowcourt Road; Great Glen (central area); Kirby Muxloe.
A comprehensive list is available from Leicestershire County Council, County Hall, Glenfield, Leicester, LE3 8RF.

Appendix 5
FAMILY HOMES AND BUSINESSMEN

This is not a comprehensive list but it gives some sense of the concentration of the middle classes in the major suburbs of Stoneygate, Oadby and Kirby Fields. The symbol (*) indicates that the property has been demolished. We are grateful to Derek Seaton for information on the businessmen of London Road (Stoneygate).

STONEYGATE EAST	Thomas Almond	Cheese/butter	Westview
	Joseph Burgess	Elastic webbing	Woodbank*
	J. Wallis Goddard	Silver plate polish	Lyndwood*
	Sir Israel Hart	Clothing	Ashleigh*
	Francis Hewitt Snr. & Jnr.	Prop., "Leicester Mercury"	Southernhay*
	Thomas William Hodges	Elastic webbing	Mayfield*
	Thomas Fielding Johnson Snr.	Wool spinning	Brookfield
	William Longmore	Brewing	Hazeldene
	William Raven	Hosiery	Portland House
	John Stafford	Cigars	Elmsleigh*
	James Went	Head, Wyggeston Boys Sch.	Gapfield
STONEYGATE WEST	James Batten	Corn & coal merchant	Sefton House
	John Wycliffe Black	Footwear	The Elms*
	Thomas Henry Bowell	Architect & surveyor	Ventnor
	Herbert H. Burton	Rubber	Quarrington
	Robert Curtis	Jewellery	Edina
	William Jesse Freer	Solicitor	The Stoney Gate*
	Harry Simpson Gee	Footwear	Knighton Frith*
	Robert Geoffrey Kemp	Hosiery	Swynford
	Thomas Lawrence	Footwear	The Oaks*
	John Leavesley	Footwear	Brackendale
	Edward Cave Moore	Hosiery	Branksome
	Sir Jonathan North	Footwear	Brackendale
	John D. Nowell	Railway contractor	The Cedars*
	Sir Frederick Oliver	Footwear	The Firs
	T.W. Pettifer	Architect	Broomhills*
	John Raven	Hosiery	Buckhurst*
	James Roberts	Grocery & provisions	Ivanhoe Villas
	John Alfred Spriggs	Editor, Leicester Mail	Eversley
	William Stevenson	Footwear	Pen-Silva
	Thomas Eric Toller	Solicitor	Stoneygate House*
	Sir Thomas Wright	Solicitor	The Hollies*
	Gerald Davis Wykes	Printing	Snaithingholm

OADBY	John Bolton	Hosiery	Tetuan
	F.S. Brice	Hosiery	Middlemeade
	Miss W. L. Fox	Confectionery	The Knoll
	Duncan Henderson	Footwear	Glebe House
	Ernest Lillie	Elastic webbing	Manorcroft
	Alexander Lorrimer	Hosiery	Sorrento
	William Winterton	Brick manufacture	The Knoll
KIRBY FIELDS	Ralph Waldo Bedingfield	Architect	Ringwood
	Henry Swain Bennett	Solicitor	Holmewood
	Matthew Brady	Footwear	Lara House
	John Bolton	Hosiery	East Leigh
	George Lawton Brown	Architect	Elmcroft*
	A.W. Crane	Doctor	Forest View
	Septimus Green	Footwear	Muckross
	Thomas Hollis	Timber	The Barncroft
	Frank Page Hopps	Accountant	Wahnfried
	George H. Hughes	Yarn merchant	Highfields
	Frank Hewitt Jnr.	Prop., "Leicester Mercury"	Walburton*
	G. Crawford Johnson	Department stores (Joseph Johnson)	The Holt*
	William Wheeler Kendall	Umbrellas	Moel Llys
	Robert Pochin	Ironmonger	Elmstead
	Edward Percy Rose	Dentist	The Spinneys
	James Turner	Leather	Fernleigh
	Sir Edward Wood	Footwear	Sunnydene

BIBLIOGRAPHY

Primary sources (including theses & dissertations)

ADW Partnership (architects), Leicester: archive

Deeds of properties of current property owners

Evington Echo, No.13 (January 1983) and No.14 (March 1983)

Freer D., "Business families in Victorian Leicester", M.Phil, University of Leicester (1975)

Goddard Archive, courtesy of Anthony Goddard

Leicester Confederation of Builders, Minutes

Leicester Mercury

Pick Everard (architects), Leicester: archive

Oral Histories of property owners/businessmen/builders

Roberts P., "Stockdale Harrison and Sons", unpublished dissertation, University of Sheffield (1986)

Warner Sheppard and Wade, sale brochures 1920s & 30s

Wright's Directory of Leicestershire & Rutland

BOOKS AND PAMPHLETS
General sources

Anthony J., The Gardens of Britain, Vol. 6: "The East Midlands" (1979)

Blomfield. R. & Thomas I. S., The Formal Garden in England (1892; repr. 1985)

Briggs A., Victorian Cities (1990 edn.)

Cumming E. & Kaplan W., Arts and Crafts Movement (1991)

Curl J. S., Victorian Architecture (1990 edn.)

Durant S., C. F. A. Voysey, (Architectural Monograph No.19, 1992)

Girouard M., Sweetness and Light: the 'Queen Anne Movement' 1860-1900 (1977)

Haigh D., Baillie Scott - The Artistic House (1995)

Jellicoe G, & Jellicoe S., The Landscape of Man (1975)

Long H., The Edwardian House: the middle class home in Britain 1880-1914 (1993)

Ottewill D., The Edwardian Garden (1989)

Raynor J., The Middle Class (1969)

Robinson W., The Wild Garden (1870); The English Flower Garden (1883)

Scott-James A., The Cottage Garden (1981)

Thorne R., "Building Bridges: George Godwin and architectural journalism", in Marsden G. ed., Victorian Values (1990)

Tunnard C., Gardens in the Modern Landscape (1938)

Local sources

Pick Everard: 125 Years (1992)

Bennett J. D., "Victorian and Edwardian Buildings of Leicestershire", Transactions of the Leicestershire Archeological and Historical Society, LIX (1984-5)

Boynton H., Λ Prospect of Oadby (1993)

Brandwood G. & Cherry M., The Goddards and Six Generations of Architects (1990)

Broad J. N., Glenfield Hospital Leicester, 1906-1982 (1982)

Farquhar J., Arthur Wakerley 1862-1931 (1984)

Gill R., The Book of Leicester (1985)

Halford E., The Grand Old Man: Before and After (1984)

Jopp K., Corah of Leicester 1815-1965 (1965)

Kirkham P., Harry Peach: Dryad and the DIA (1986)

Leicester City Council, In search of an Architect: Arthur Wakerley town trail (1975)

Leicester City Council, The Quality of Leicester (1994)

Leicester Mercury, Transport Memories of Leicestershire (1990)

Mullins S. & Griffiths G., Cap and Apron: an oral history of domestic service in the shires 1880-1950 (1986)

Rice R. J., "The Quaternary Deposits of Central Leicestershire", Philosophical Transactions of the Royal Society of London (15 February 1968)

Simmons J., Life in Victorian Leicester (1971)

Smith L. Lloyd & Keene R. J. B., The First Hundred Years of the Leicestershire and Rutland Society of Architects (1972)

Smith M. ed., Bygone Birstall (1988)

Sturgess-Wells H., Milestones and Memories (1956)

Wilshire J., Old Kirby Muxloe (1986)

INDEX

ARCHITECTS